Mindfully Happy

Waking up to Life

Diane Lang

Printed in the United States of America
ISBN 978-0-9987874-0-4

Table of Contents

Cultivating Happiness

Happiness depends upon ourselves.

—Aristotle

To start cultivating your mindfully happy life, you must ask yourself:

Is my life happy? Am I happy?

How do I define happiness?

What does happiness look like to me? What does it feel like?

In each area of my life, what brings me happiness?

Am I appreciating my day and all it involves? Am I grateful for everything I have?

Am I being my authentic self? Am I living the life I want — the key word being "I"?

What we know about happiness is that it involves having an appreciation for what we have and where we are. It also involves looking forward to the future, growing, changing, and trying to be our best. It's the experience of joy. ("Joy" is a state of great delight and/or happiness.) It's a feeling that our lives have meaning. The mix of gratitude for what we have and striving to be our best is a good foundation for happiness.

Happiness is also an individual thing. We all have different definitions of happiness, but if you don't know what brings you happiness, how can you get there? I have my clients write a list of five to ten things that bring them happiness. My suggestion is to divide the list into different areas of your life, writing down what brings you happiness at home, career, relationships, etc. You want a well-balanced life. If you find you get most of your happiness from one area, then you will be stressed and unhappy if that changes. For example, if your work is the only area of your life that brings you happiness and then you get laid off or fired, you will find yourself without any joy. If you have a balanced life where you find happiness in different areas of your life, then you can still feel happy when one area is lacking. Remember, the list is for you only. It's not what brings others happiness, what society says makes us happy, etc. It's your list and must come from your authentic self.

After you write the list (which can be harder than you imagine), look at your life and see if you do any of the things that bring you happiness. I had a client say to me that happiness is a warm bath, with soft music and bath salts. It sounds relaxing, soothing, and like a completely mindful experience. When I asked my client when the last time she took a bath was, she couldn't remember. It was so long ago. If what brings you happiness is not incorporated into your schedule, how do you expect to be happier? You need to schedule what brings you happiness just like you would play dates for your kids, assignments that need to be done at work, etc. Your happiness has to be included in your life. Happiness needs to be a priority.

Happiness Scale

Negative default is our natural setting. This is both bad and good. It helps us to notice when we feel threatened and unsafe. It helps us learn from bad experiences. Unfortunately, many people end up staying in their negative setting. The good news is that we can be happier than where we are today—but first we need to know our starting point.

Where do you find yourself on the happiness scale of one to ten, one being the least happy and ten being the happiest? Don't ask about today. Ask in general. In the last few months, where have you been? Ask yourself that question and be honest. Most of my clients and students say around a six or seven, but I have had people ask, "Can I be a zero on a scale of one to ten?" "Can I be a negative number?" You can be any place you truly feel you are. Don't judge it. Use it as a starting point and work your way up.

Once you have your starting place, ask yourself where you want to be. Is the number you want to achieve realistic? You can't go from a one to a ten, but you could go from a one to a three in a reasonable amount of time. Your number has to be realistic. We always make changes in baby steps. Our happiness levels can change due to circumstances. That is normal and to be expected.

Whether or not you're feeling happy right now, you can always be happier and more resilient. When we are optimistic, we have the ability to recover from challenges quickly. Happier people don't let failures and mistakes stop them; instead they work to overcome them. The more optimistic you are, the more resilient you are.

We all have a genetic set point of happiness. Some people are happier than others naturally, but no matter what level of happiness you have, you can always increase it. There are some simple habits we can create in our lives to feel happier pretty quickly. In this book, we will go over a variety of different happiness habits and mindfulness tips that will help you to feel happier and be more resilient. Follow these happiness habits and make them a daily routine. We know that we can't live a stress-free life. There will be circumstances that will be outside of our control, but we can be resilient so that when the stressful times come (and they will), you will have built a strong foundation that will allow you to move through these times more quickly and smoothly.

Happiness is a commitment and a choice. Before you move on to the rest of the chapters in this book, make sure you're ready to make the commitment to yourself, and to take the time to add happiness into your life. Happiness is available to everyone. We can all be happier than we are today, but that means making it a priority. This includes self-care and some work. If you're ready, then continue on to cultivate your happiness.

Happiness is largely an attitude of mind, of viewing life from the right angle.

—Dale Carnegie

Benefits of Happiness

Happiness has been correlated with better health, in both individuals and communities. Some studies suggest that states of happiness may be associated with lower stress-related hormones and better immune function. Happy people are less likely to suffer from depression. Happier people can live longer and healthier lives.

Happy people are more creative and productive at work. When you are happy, you have more energy and are able to have better focus and concentration. Happy people are also more successful at work.

Happy people feel more satisfied in their lives and can see situations from a positive perspective, so even when stressful events happen, they can see the bigger picture and know everything will be OK. They think, "I can get through this!"

Remember happiness is contagious: spending a lot of time with happy people can make you happier.

All the benefits of happiness speak for themselves.

A Surefire Recipe for Success

Most of my clients have families and full-time jobs, so adding more habits to their lives can seem overwhelming at first. This is why I have my clients add in one new habit a month. This gives the person time to get comfortable with the habit and time for it to stick.

My suggestion—pick one habit for each month and stick with it for the month. Even if you have a day or two where you forget or skip it, just continue on the next day without judgment. Do this for a month, and then you can add in another new habit for a month. This usually works for my clients without any added stress, just more happiness.

I have been practicing these habits for years now, and the benefits are huge. Gratitude made the biggest impact on me. After I started doing gratitude, it took about three months to notice a change. I still remember the "aha" moment. I was driving to work on a cold, rainy day in rush hour, and I got stuck in major traffic. At first I started my usual rant about traffic, I got frustrated, and my anger levels were rising, when all of a sudden I started reciting my gratitude. I was grateful that I was safe, warm, and able to call my office, and I realized it was all going to be just fine. That's the power of gratitude.

I have heard similar stories from my clients. One client said the daily routine of writing down her gratitude and what good happened that day changed the noise in her head that used to keep her up at night. Her sleep improved. All of the habits in this book have completely changed my life for the better. My overall health and happiness have improved. I know if they worked for me and my clients, they can work for you.

We must be willing to get rid of the life we've planned, so as to have the life that is waiting for us.

—Joseph Campbell

Mindfully Happy Habits

Action may not always bring happiness; but there is no happiness without action.

—Benjamin Disraeli

Mindfully Happy Habit #1—Are Your Basic Needs Met?

Many people feel blah, low energy, fatigued, and unbalanced. I have had clients come to me thinking they need counseling or coaching due to these symptoms. What I have realized is some of my clients don't need coaching. They need to have their basic needs met.

I have most of my clients keep a "Journal of Truth" for one week. It is similar to keeping a food diary. It's writing everything down. There are no changes to be made during that week; it's just keeping track of four things: food, water, sleep, and exercise.

1. **Food journal**—what did you eat and when? Many of us don't eat well. We have heard the expression "you are what you eat," and that is true. Unfortunately, many of us eat foods that are high in sugar, low in nutrition, processed, or low-fat/fat-free foods that use fake sugars. This type of diet can cause us to feel fatigued, low energy, blah, and sluggish, and to have low concentration levels. We also need to watch *when* we eat. If we go too long without food, we can feel shaky, irritable, and moody. Changing our diets can change our lives. Reading food labels can help declutter our kitchen and change our lifestyle. Two great tips:

   - If the first two ingredients are sugar or fake sugar, it's time to remove it from the kitchen.

- If you can't pronounce any of the ingredients on the label, it's time to remove it from the kitchen.

2. **Water**—how much water do you drink each day? This does not include coffee, soda, or tea, unless it's herbal, decaffeinated tea, or broth. Most of us feel fatigued and low energy sometimes, and this can be due to a lack of water in our diet. I had a client who would feel sluggish around three o'clock while at work. She typically would go for a cup of coffee or grab a soda. She would sometimes go to the vending machine for a pick-me-up snack. I had her exchange all of that for two glasses of water at that time. Within a few weeks, she had more energy in the afternoon without any added calories, sugar, or caffeine. Try it! Carry a water bottle with you to add more water to your day. Be hydrated and see the changes.

3. **Sleep**—how much sleep do you get at night? Most Americans get four to six hours of sleep per night, when we need around eight hours. If we go three nights with six hours' sleep or less, cognitively it's like not sleeping for 24 hours. Our attention span, focus, concentration, moods, and memory are all off.

Sleep hygiene tips

- Stay regular—try to go sleep at around the same time every night and wake up around the same time every day, even on weekends and during time off.
- Avoid caffeine, nicotine, large meals, and alcohol for at least five to six hours before bed. They can all interrupt your sleep.
- Sleep routine—set up a few things you do at night to signal that it's time for sleep. I have some clients who have a cup of chamomile tea and do some stretches before bed.

- Bedroom—keep it cool, quiet, and dark. We sleep the best this way.
- Sleep when you're actually tired. If we spend time in bed wide-awake, we will find ourselves staring at the clock and becoming frustrated.
- Write out a to do list before going to sleep. This will help you to avoid those ruminating thoughts about the busyness of the next day. We can sleep better when we get the thoughts and worry out of our heads.

4. **Exercise**—did you exercise today? Exercise is a great way to produce endorphins (the happy chemical) while reducing cortisol (a stress hormone). For emotional health, if we walk four times a week for thirty minutes, we can get feelings similar to taking an antidepressant. Any exercise is great. I hit the gym a few times a week, but on those days when I can't, I wear a pedometer and try to get ten thousand steps in. A pedometer is a great investment. For ten to twenty dollars, you can find out how many steps and miles you walked and how many calories you burned. Just wearing the pedometer motivates me to walk more.

At the end of the week, read through your journal. You can see what is unbalanced in your life and what areas to work on. Then you can make the changes accordingly. When people have their basic needs met, they feel better physically and emotionally. Remember, your mind and body are strongly linked. If your emotional health is down, it affects your body. If your physical health starts to decline, it could make you feel emotionally down. To have total health, we must have a healthy mind and body.

Stats:

- Two-thirds of all office visits to your family doctor are related to stress, says the American Academy of Family Physicians.

- The World Health Organization (WHO) states, "There is no physical health without mental health."
- People whose glasses are half full are reportedly twice as likely to have healthy hearts, according to a new study published in the *Health Behavior and Policy Review Journal.*

Mindfully Happy Habit #2—Gratitude

Joy is what happens to us when we allow ourselves to recognize how good things really are.

—Marianne Williamson

I added gratitude to my daily routine about three years ago, and it is the best habit I have ever formed. Gratitude is a form of meditation, so you get all the benefits of meditation, such as lowering stress levels, finding calm and a sense of peace, living in the moment, better sleep, and much more. Remember, meditation is the best natural way to de-stress. Gratitude is also a great way to retrain your brain to think positively. Gratitude allows us to see the good in our lives.

We humans tend to always see and focus on the negative. We have "negative blinders" on. When we add gratitude to our daily routine, we start seeing things from a positive perspective. It shows us all what we have that we never pay attention to. A client told me, "Gratitude allowed me to see what was right in front of me." Gratitude gives us a sense of appreciation and thanks for what we have.

I have my clients do a "gratitude check" daily. Each day, they take a few minutes to either say or write down two or three things they are grateful for. We don't want to get in a gratitude rut where we keep saying the same things over and over, or where we say gratitude without having any meaning behind it. For gratitude to work, you need to really take some time to think about what you are truly grateful for. What are those things? You can also dig deeper into your gratitude by asking why you're grateful for those things and list the reasons. For many, keeping a gratitude journal is very effective. It's your choice when or how you do it. Just do it.

Create a list of all the things you are truly grateful for in your life. After your write the list, look at the list and ask yourself, "Do I appreciate these things or take them for granted?" This list helps you to be more mindful of the good in your life. It makes you self-aware.

Show your gratitude to someone else. Say thank you. Expressing your gratitude to others is another way to feel grateful. I have my clients send a note of thanks once a week. In today's technological world, it has become a very easy thing to do. You can send a quick e-mail or text letting someone you love know how much you appreciate him or her. It's always best to do it face-to-face or at least through phone communication, but if you can't do that, you have many options now to express your gratitude.

Benefits of Gratitude

1. Gratitude improves physical health—the more grateful you are, the more likely you are to take good care of your health. Grateful people tend to exercise regularly and have frequent medical checkups.
2. Gratitude improves emotional health—it reduces negative emotions such as envy, resentment, and frustration, while improving your happiness levels.
3. Gratitude reduces social comparison—it gives us the ability to appreciate other people's success and accomplishments while reducing our need to compare ourselves to others. This is a huge benefit in a world filled with FOMO (fear of missing out) due to increased use of the Internet and social media.
4. Gratitude and sleep—doing your gratitude checks at night can help you sleep better. If you go to sleep after gratitude, you're going to bed with positive thoughts that will help you wake up in a good mood.
5. Gratitude and bouncing back—when we are grateful, we can see the big picture. Even if we have a bad situation or a stressful day, we can see all the good we have in our lives and how this stressful situation will pass.
6. Gratitude and optimism—grateful people tend to be more optimistic. Optimism has a positive impact on our bodies, boosting our immune system.
7. Gratitude allows us to see what's in front of us. It helps us to enjoy the little things, which we tend to overlook and take for granted. By helping us to see the good in every day, we cultivate more happiness.
8. Retrain your brain for success—when you are grateful, you start noticing the good instead of the bad. In a world filled with negativity and fear, it's easier to notice all the bad in the world, but with gratitude you can also see the good. One of the best benefits of gratitude for me was the capability to see the good and bad in every situation. It also improves your resiliency. Recognizing how much you have to be thankful for fosters resiliency.

Mindfully Happy Habit # 3—Random Acts of Kindness

One of the best ways to instantly feel better and happier is to perform a random act of kindness for someone else. Random acts of kindness motivate us to be better people and inspire us to believe that people are good. They also result in a significant improvement in immune system function. They help reduce stress and chronic pain and help us have a better night's rest. It's a win-win situation. When we do a random act of kindness, we get a boost of happiness that lasts for twenty-four to seventy-two hours. The person we do the act of kindness for also receives a boost of happiness. It also boosts our, and their, self-esteem. Paying it forward is a great way to keep our levels of happiness up while helping others, but there are some obstacles that can stop us from feeling good.

1. When you do a random act of kindness, it must be done with no expectation. When we do something nice for others (especially people we know) we tend to want to receive a thank-you or some kind of appreciation. Unfortunately, that is not always the case. So, if you want to do a random act of kindness, it needs to be done because you want to do it. We should not be expecting a pat on the back or a thank-you. Just doing the act should be enough reward for us. This can be tough because when we do acts of kindness for others and receive no acknowledgment, we can feel hurt and upset. But, if we do it with no expectation, we can walk away knowing we did the right thing for the right reason.

2. Money does not have to be involved. Money doesn't buy us a lot of happiness unless our basic needs aren't met. If we need money for basics such as food, clothing, or shelter, then adding more money to our lives will bring happiness. *But*, if our basic needs are met, adding more money won't change our happiness levels by much. So, you don't need to pay for someone's coffee or lunch to "pay it forward." It can be as simple as holding the door open or giving up your seat on a bus.

3. A random act of kindness is a great way to be a positive parent—being a positive parent is all about being a role model for your kids. Kids learn through role modeling, imitation, and example. Every time our kids see their parents do a random act of kindness, it teaches them to follow suit. It's a great way to teach by example.

4. David R. Hamilton, a chemist who now studies happiness, says that performing a kind act releases oxytocin—the same brain chemical that surges when you hold or snuggle your baby, which also temporarily lowers blood pressure. "Kindness is literally good for your heart," explains Hamilton. Great news for all of us. We can help others while keeping a healthy heart. Bonus!

Great Ideas for Random Acts of Kindness

1. Bring your neighbor's newspaper to the front door with some homemade cookies, cupcakes, etc.

2. Be a kind driver—curb your road rage, let someone have your parking spot, let the next car into the lane, etc.

3. Leave a good-morning note for your family. My husband does this a lot. He will leave a note just saying, "Have a good day, love you." You can do this for a friend or family member with a text or e-mail.

4. Waiting at the supermarket, but not in a rush? Let the person behind you go first!

5. Send thank-you notes to heroes such as the military, policeman, fireman, nurses, etc.

6. Does your child have a great teacher? Send a thank-you note to school with a special treat like a candle or Hershey's Kisses.

7. Donate your old clothes, books, and jewelry to your local church or synagogue. Have your kids do the same with their old books, toys, stuffed animals, etc. As long as the stuff is in good shape, you will be helping someone.

8. Bake or buy food for your local food bank or pantry.
9. Send someone an e-card saying "Thank you" or "I love you" for no reason.
10. Give a compliment, a smile, an extra hug, a wink, a kiss, etc.

The one thing we can never get enough of is love. And the one thing we never give enough of is love.

—Henry Miller

We make a living by what we get. We make a life by what we give.

—Sir Winston Churchill

Mindfully Happy Habit #4—Noticing the Good

This is a two-part habit. Every day, write or say three to five things you like about yourself—most women tell me this is the toughest part. They can give me a list of ten things they don't like about themselves, but to say nice things to ourselves seems awkward and uncomfortable. So, start with one or two things if that's all you have, but keep at it. The list will grow, I promise. For this habit, it can be anything—personality traits, how you responded to a situation, how you were a positive role model as a parent, your job, etc. If you can't think of at least three things, then always find at least one. Sometimes I can only find one good thing about myself, but after I take some time to find that one thing, more pop up.

In the beginning, this can be a hard exercise because you may be starting off with low self-esteem. That's OK. All that means is this exercise will help you build it. This habit will retrain your brain to see the good in yourself. Start small with one thing each day if that's all you have, but it will grow, and so will the love you have for yourself. If you're still having trouble, you can ask people close to you what they like best about you. Their answers might surprise you and teach you a little something about yourself.

The second part of this habit is for the end of the day. Write or say three to five things that were positive in your day or that you did well. It could be as simple as the weather or an act of self-care. There is no judgment. Make sure to say different things each day if you can. When coming up with what was so good today, really dive deep into it. Think about why it was so good. Really be mindful of your day and look for the positives.

We tend to notice the bad. For example, you could be having a really great day and then one little thing happened that wasn't so great—what do you pay attention to at the end of the day? The one negative. That's the negative default rearing its ugly head again. But sometimes a bad situation could end up being the best thing that happened all day because it taught you a valuable lesson and caused you to grow or make changes. Being mindful will help you see the good even in a bad situation. Sometimes it will be hard to find things that were good; we all have those days. If that is the case, it's OK to just have one good thing. That one thing could be "Thank God I made it through this day!"

Patience is key to all of these happiness habits, but especially to this one. When we try to start noticing the good in ourselves and our lives, we can get frustrated. Most of us naturally see the negative. It's the negative blinders. For example, I have a client who will come to me and say, "My whole life sucks!" When I ask why, they tell me one thing that went wrong that day: they got a flat tire, they got a bad grade at school, or they didn't get their bonus at work. What we do is take that one bad thing and exaggerate it into a huge event. The one bad thing turns into "My whole life sucks."

When this happens, I ask my clients to tell me what is going well in their life. Most answer "Nothing" or "How could you ask me that now?" What I usually do then is ask them some questions such as:

How is your health?

How is your family's health?

Do you have good relationships? Good families? Support systems?

Do you have a house? Clothes? Food? Car?

This starts bringing us back to reality and an understanding that even when something bad happens, there is still good. We need to balance the negative with the positive.

18

The two habits above will do this for you, but you must make it through the month before giving up. The first week or two, you will feel awkward and uncomfortable, and will probably laugh at yourself when you start saying the three to five things that you like about yourself. You might even feel fake and think you're lying to yourself. That is all OK and normal! But, if you keep working through it, you will eventually realize that there are good things about you and your life, so don't give up. I think it took me about two weeks before I believed anything I said about myself, but somewhere in week three I realized, "Wow, I'm not so bad. I actually do like my kindness, caring, and empathetic personality." That was my "AHA!" moment, and you will have yours if you continue.

Everyone thinks of changing the world, but no one thinks of changing himself.

—Leo Tolstoy

Nurture your mind with great thoughts, for you will never go higher than you think.

—Benjamin Disraeli

We can always choose to perceive things differently. You can focus on what's wrong with your life or you can focus on what's right.

—Marianne Williamson

Mindfully Happy Habit #5—Meditation

I can't begin to say enough about meditation. It's very hard to define, but mediation to me is a state of awareness and peace, and a step in the process of spiritual transformation. Meditation is one of the most effective ways to naturally de-stress. Meditation has truly been a life changer for me. Remember, mediation is a practice, something we intentionally set out to do. Mindfulness is a general sense of the present moment. We will go into a mindful lifestyle later on in this book. Here are some great reasons to try and benefits of meditation.

- Lowers high blood pressure.
- Lowers the levels of blood lactate, reducing anxiety attacks.
- Decreases any tension-related pain such as tension headaches, ulcers, insomnia, muscle, and joint problems.
- Increases serotonin production, which improves mood and behavior.
- Improves the immune system.
- Increases energy level.
- Increases creativity.
- Increases happiness.
- Increases emotional stability—the ability to maintain stability and balance during stressful circumstances.
- Gives clarity and peace of mind, a sense of calmness and relaxation.
- Reduces pain levels dramatically and enhances ability to cope with pain that may not go away.
- Sharpens the mind for better focus and concentration.
- Instills a greater enthusiasm for life.

Many of my clients will say, "I can't meditate" or "I can't clear my mind." We must remember not to judge ourselves. There is no right or wrong in meditation. If you can have a few moments of quiet time, you're on the right track. Don't set up any expectations on your meditative experience. Each time you meditate, the experience will be different. Some meditative experiences can bring up negative feelings. The best way to get through this is to feel the emotions but don't analyze them. They will eventually diminish. If you keep having recurring memories and/or emotions come up, it might be a sign that you need to work through it with a therapist.

Will you still have thoughts that come up, sounds you hear, etc.? Of course, that's natural. Just let them be and go back to focusing on your breathing or mantra. Stop resisting the thoughts and let them just flow. I have some clients who picture their thoughts floating away in clouds. I think of a speaker system with the big, round volume nob and that I'm slowly turning it down to off. This lowers the volume of my sounds. We know the inner voice is still there, along with sounds in the environment, but we just don't pay much attention to them.

Some people feel restlessness when trying to meditate. This is normal; it takes time for our bodies to relax and slow down, especially if you're meditating after a full day of activity. Continue through the restlessness. Be aware of the feeling, the sensations it brings in your body. You can make the meditation experience be about feeling the restlessness. It will eventually calm down.

A great way to start meditating is by using guided meditations. If you get a pair of headphones to plug into your mobile device, you can try using a guided meditation. All you need to do is go to YouTube.com and type in "guided meditations," and millions will come up. You can choose a meditation by amount of time, type, people, etc. For some people, just having sounds of rain, nature, or the beach is enough. Others like someone guiding them through the meditation. All or any of those are fine. You can start off with a quick guided meditation that goes for five to seven minutes and work your way up to fifteen minutes. For some, starting with three to five minutes is best and can feel like forever. You can be seated in a chair, cross-legged on the floor, or laying down. If you're sitting, make sure your spine is upright. If you're laying down, you might fall asleep during your meditation, but don't judge. If you fell asleep, you probably needed it. You can do a walking meditation or a writing morning meditation. The best thing is to just start. The longer we do it, the better chance we have to continue meditating as part of our daily routine. Just give it a shot!

Realize deeply that the present moment is all you ever have.

—Eckhart Tolle

Inside myself is a place where I live all alone. That's where you renew your springs that never dry up.

—Pearl S. Buck

Mindfully Happy Habit #6—Taking Risks and Stepping Outside Your Comfort Zone

Your comfort zone is a place where you feel mentally safe and secure. It's where you follow a routine and schedule that minimizes stress and risk-taking. It's a place we naturally tend to go back to over and over again.

Let's think about what would happen if we challenged ourselves to feel a little stress and risk by stepping outside the box?

I have my clients ask themselves these questions before they start their day:

> *How can I step outside of my comfort zone today?*
>
> *How can I challenge myself today?*
>
> *What small thing can I do today that is outside my norm?*
>
> *What one thing can I do that makes me feel both a little nervous and a little excited at the same time?*

Most of my clients express a feeling in their stomach both of nerves and excitement when they stretch outside their comfort zone. When you feel that little twinge in your stomach, you know you're stepping outside the box you built for yourself. The box that is very secure and safe. The box where you know what to expect and what you will feel. There will be no surprises there, but that also means no growth. A lot of people talk about feeling stuck. This is common. People feel stuck, stale, and/or stagnate. This means we are not growing and moving forward. We are not challenging ourselves. We need to challenge ourselves and take risks to move forward and grow both professionally and personally. When we are stuck, it's very hard to be creative and productive, so all areas of our lives suffer.

Most of us fear change, which is why we stay in our safe little boxes, but let's have an honest discussion about change. Change is the one constant in the world. We can't stop it. Many things are outside of our control, such as weather, natural disasters, terror attacks, the economy, accidents, aging, loss of loved ones, etc. Even if I stay in my comfort zone and never step outside of it, the world around me changes. So, even if I decide to never change, keep the same job, stay in the same house, drive the same car, wear the same clothes, etc., my life will still change. The best way to deal with change is to embrace it. If we fight it and resist change, we will cause excessive worrying and stress. If we accept that change is a part of life, it's easier to deal with change as it happens. Another way to embrace change is to change how we perceive it. I personally love most change because it feels like a new opportunity, a fresh start. I think of each day as a reboot. "I wonder what today will bring" is my motto.

For example, aging (not a big fan) is reality. I can fight it all I want, but the years keep coming and the physical changes happen. I can dye the gray hair, but it's still there. I can get Botox, but the wrinkles will come. Aging is a natural process, and all the fighting and resistance won't change it, but it can make the process even harder. If we keep fighting and resisting it, it will become the focus of our attention. It will become our identity. Then we will feel the effects of age, even if they are just a side effect of our thoughts. I think I'm old, therefore I am, and all the negative that comes with aging will happen to me. What we believe about ourselves becomes our reality. True, we can't stop aging, but we can change how we react to change and how we feel about it.

I had a client in her fifties tell me she always wanted to wear a bikini but she thinks she is too old to wear one. This client had just lost fifty pounds by stepping outside her comfort zone and choosing to start running daily, and even go a step further and run a marathon. She succeeded, lost the weight, and ran the marathon. She felt great and motivated. She already stepped outside her comfort zone a few times, but now she was faced with the challenge of "the bikini in her fifties." The truth be told, this client

24

never wore a bikini even when she was younger, so the thought of it in mid-life was totally scary. We discussed it, and she decided she would wear the bikini just once and see how it felt. That was the baby step, just once at a pool with a few friends. She expressed the twinge in her stomach that I previously mentioned, so she knew she was stretching herself. What was scary and outside her box became a day full of compliments and a new part of her summer wear.

I give the example above because you can see we all have our comfort zone. We create our own boxes where we feel safe and secure, and they are different for everyone. There is no judgment or comparing. It's about challenging ourselves and growing.

What happens when we challenge ourselves and step outside the comfort zone?

1. We become more productive. The comfort zone only allows us to go so far. We remain busy in our comfort zones, but that is not a good thing. The busyness can help us to avoid trying new things or procrastinating until a later day that we are just too busy to get to.
2. Positive reinforcement—once we step outside the box and survive, we realize we can do it again. It provides momentum and motivation. Even if we don't succeed and get the result we wanted, we realize that we safely strayed from the comfort zone and nothing major happened. We realize that the stress and fear we feel is more in our heads then what really happens. Example: If I'm extremely afraid to speak in public for work but step out of my comfort zone and do it, I will feel a sense of accomplishment even if it's not the best speech. Just the fact that I conquered my fears and survived is enough to feel a sense of hope toward other small steps of risk.

3. We are happier when we have variety and try new things in life. We can take small steps into risks like trying a new food, drink, or restaurant. It doesn't have to be something huge.

   Example: I had a client who was very shy and spent her life trying to blend in. After years of this, she was getting frustrated by her lack of promotions and raises at work. She wanted to take a small step to make people notice her and step outside of her comfort zone. We decided to do this small but risky change. She would wear a bright color shirt and lipstick (she always tried to blend in, wearing black or very dark colors). The next day she wore a black pant suit with a red sweater underneath and red lipstick to match. For many, this might not be a big challenge, but for my client this was huge and caused her to feel very uncomfortable walking into work. Halfway through the day, I received a message about how employees at work were giving her compliments and saying her name. She didn't even realize some of the employees knew who she was. This was a small start to many other small changes she began making. Within a few months, she had made a few new friends, had a brighter wardrobe, and had a little more confidence. All small steps lead to positive changes.

How to Challenge Yourself

1. Every day, do something that challenges you just a little, something that causes the twinge feeling. Small things like saying "Hi" or smiling at a stranger, trying a new food, taking a different route to work, wearing a new color or perfume, taking a class, or trying a new workout class.
2. When you have to make a decision and you feel a little anxious, ask yourself: *What is making me feel uncomfortable? Is there room here to take a risk? Can I try something new here?*
3. Trust in your choices. Following your intuition can be risky for some, but it's a way to start trusting yourself and following your

gut. Really pay attention to what you're feeling physically. This can give you a few signs of what you want to do even if you're feeling anxious and nervous.

4. Take baby steps. If you're afraid of heights, don't jump on a roller coaster. Instead, take a ride on an elevator to the third or fourth floor. The next day go to the fifth floor, and so on.

5. Learn a new skill. Take a class not for college credit, but to learn a new skill and/or meet new people. Join a volunteer group, travel, etc. The happiest people keep growing both professionally and personally. We constantly stretch ourselves when we continually learn and grow.

    * This can also be trying a new hobby, like gardening, painting, singing, etc.

As much as I tell my clients to challenge themselves every day with small things, it's also important to go back to your natural comfort zone. You don't always need to be pushing your boundaries. It's great to challenge yourself and then take some time to reflect on your accomplishments and experiences. Even if it didn't turn out as expected, be proud of yourself for trying.

"Be happy for this moment. This moment is your life."

—Omar Khayyam

Mindfully Happy Habit #7—Can and Can't Control

This is a big one, especially if you have control issues, which a lot of us do. We feel the need to be in control all the time and feel anxious when we have lost control. The truth be told, we only have control over one thing: ourselves. We can control how we react and respond. We can sometimes control what situation we put ourselves in, but not all the time. The truth is, control over ourselves is all we really need. When we release the need to control others, we stop wasting energy trying to change things or complaining about them. I also have the option of letting go of control and accepting where I am at this very moment. This is a hard one for many of us to understand. I know I have been there numerous times. My most recent trip to letting go and accepting was five years ago. Let me share my story.

I have an illness that was very scary and caused me to have great difficulties swallowing food, water, and even my saliva. For months, I was losing weight and we couldn't figure out what was wrong with me. After many months of tests, a neurologist told me I had ALS (amyotrophic lateral sclerosis), also known as Lou Gehrig's disease, and to go home and get my life in order. This put me in a tailspin. I was angry, and life felt so unfair. I was completely devastated. I went home and freaked out. I had a friend come over who gave me some great advice that she received from me months ago. (I hate having my own advice thrown back in my face . . . LOL.) She said, "When you have lost complete control, the only control you have is to let go and accept where you are." This is tough, but when you let go and accept, the stress and pressure immediately lifts because your resistance is gone. You can finally breathe again and see life with more clarity.

After a night of no sleep, crying my eyes out, and releasing my control, I felt like the weight of the world was lifted off my shoulders and I was ready to accept my fate and make choices based on this acceptance. I felt at peace. A few days later I found out my true diagnosis, which was not that great, but not ALS. I still had to go through the whole letting go and accepting my new life. My new diagnosis had no cure and would change my life. This true acceptance allowed me to grieve my old life and to move forward to create my new identity. I can look back now and realize the blessings of my illness and the new life I have created, but none of this would be possible without letting go of the fight and accepting my new situation and/or identity. Those two things are under your control and affect the conscious choices you make.

How to Let Go and Accept

1. Resistance is the key factor here. We don't want to let go. We want to fight and resist the change. This is normal. Resistance is also a sign that there is pain and hurt that we still need to deal with. Once we realize and learn that all the resistance is doing is causing us more stress and suffering, we can start to let go. If your resistance is bringing pain, you will need to feel before you let go.

2. Think of the consequences of holding on to stress and anxiety both physically and emotionally. For some of my clients, just being aware of the serious health consequences is enough to start the process.

3. Make the decision to let go. This puts you in control. You have a choice to keep resisting or to let go. By making the decision to let go, you have made the decision to move forward and accept your situation. By letting go and accepting, you have made your happiness and healing a priority.

4. Feel and express the emotions that come with letting go and accepting. Don't push your emotions away or label them as good or bad. They are your emotions without a label or judgment. It's natural to have them. For me, I cried all night. I expressed my fear and anger to my friend and husband. Feeling and expressing let me see my situation with clarity. It allowed me to move forward in awareness and ask myself the questions:
    What changes do I need to make? Will I let my illness and all that comes with it be part of my identity? How can I take a role in my new identity?

5. Letting go means to let go of the past and start living in the present. When you're in the moment, you are your happiest. When you find yourself stuck in the past, say out loud or to yourself, "Stop!" This will be your sign to come back to the present moment. Some of my clients find it more effective to visualize a stop sign. You could choose whatever word or visualization works

for you. The more you practice this technique, the more aware you become.

6. How you decide to let go and accept is up to you. Some choose to distance themselves and take a break to relax and find themselves. They take time to reevaluate their lives and where they want to go. Some of my clients say the best way to let go and accept is through meditation, learning to silence the noise and go within. Some choose the route of counseling. It doesn't matter how you do it; just making the choice is the beginning of the journey.

*Remember that accepting your situation doesn't mean you have to like it. It just means you're accepting what you can't change. Accepting what you can't change is courageous work, but it will allow for a healthier and happier life.

True happiness is . . . to enjoy the present, without anxious dependence upon the future.
—Lucius Annaeus Seneca

Meaning and Happiness

In a world filled with social media and so much focus put on being the best, a lot of us find ourselves feeling less than and trying to fit into the mold of success according to society. Even though success is an individual thing, society sets the standard and a lot of people try to reach these standards even though it affects their happiness levels. Don't get wrapped up in the notion that meaning must be something huge like being famous. We don't find more meaning because of a paycheck or a title. What we do becomes more meaningful when we realize we impacted someone's life in a positive way. It's the thank you notes, the smiles, the hugs and the words of appreciation that brings us deep meaning.

You can be happy without having meaning in your life. Most people will tell you if they are happy, but don't have meaning, their life feels shallow or they just feel like something is missing. The best is to have both; it makes our life more fulfilling and rich. When we do things that are meaningful, they don't always bring us happiness, such as being a caretaker. It gives us purpose and a sense of doing the right thing. This makes us feel proud and is something we want to teach our kids, but happiness doesn't always come from those moments. These moments create who you are as a person and who you want to be.

We can find meaning in two different ways. Finding a deeper meaning in life with such questions as:

Why am I here? What is my legacy? What's my purpose?

These are important questions in the big picture. We need to have meaning and purpose in our lives to give us a sense of direction, help us to pick the right career, lead us toward our interests, and shape how we want to help the world.

We can also find meaning in our daily lives. Ask yourself the following questions:

How can I make a difference in small ways throughout my day? How can I spread more love, kindness and warmth? How can I touch someone's life today?

To find meaning in your daily life, look at each day as a day filled with possibilities and opportunities to use your gifts, make someone smile, make someone's day a little easier, connect with others, and contribute to humankind in small ways.

For some, work gives them a sense of purpose and meaning. For others, work pays for their purpose. I have a client who wants to rescue animals but needs money to see the dream come to fruition. She strongly believes her purpose is to care for stray animals. Her job allows her to live out her purpose, which brings her great joy and meaning.

If you know the purpose of your life (which gives your life meaning) then you must ask yourself: Are you living in accordance to your purpose?

True meaning in life means to take your purpose and share it with others. When you know your purpose, you need to continue to grow, learn, and challenge yourself by taking risks; this keeps our purpose fresh and exciting.

I work with clients who have been through major trauma and have survived. One of the things most of them say is that they knew life would eventually end but it seemed so far away. They always thought they would have more time until they came close to losing it all. This is when they realized they wanted to live a life filled with meaning. Whether it meant through family, work, charity/volunteer, etc., they just knew how important it was to leave a legacy and also live the legacy while they were here.

These same clients expressed that almost losing your life makes you realize how special each moment is. Each moment is a gift. We take advantage of life; we don't appreciate the beauty that surrounds us, the joy of family and friends, the loyalty of our pets, etc. We need to learn these lessons before it's too late. This is the time to find meaning.

To find meaning in your life, a good place to start is with these questions:

What's important to me?

What do I care about? What could I talk about forever, teach or advocate for?

What changes do I want to see in the world? What problems do I want to solve?

Who do I want to be? What kind of person? What would make me proud of myself?

Here are some tips to bring a sense of meaning to your life.

1. Give – give in a way that brings a sense of meaning. What do you care about? If you care about animals then become a volunteer at your local animal shelter. It doesn't matter how you give – volunteer, charity, etc. It's just the act of caring about something strongly and taking action.

2. Connect – having meaningful relationships with people you love is so important. The more time you invest in relationships, the more meaningful they will become. This will mean being vulnerable and open. If not, we can miss out on the most meaningful and deep relationships.

3. Don't be a drifter in life – live a meaningful life. What's your purpose? Your gifts? Are you using them? Are you contributing to the world? What legacy do you want to leave?

4. Be mindful – when we are mindful and present in the moment, we can truly enjoy the moment and find meaning. We can do this when we are mindful in evaluating our lives, mindful in how we spend our time and whom we spend it with. Being mindful allows you to ask the questions: What's important to me? What gives my life meaning? Purpose?

5. Live your dreams – if we let fear win, then we will spend our lives wishing we had done things differently and in deep regret. Take actions that can make your dreams a reality.

6. Know your value – if we are not aware of all the good we do in the world, we won't feel meaning. I had a client who is a teacher but never knew the impact she had on the kids. Even though the students would give her compliments and great evaluations, she still didn't recognize her hard work or value. Your life could have great meaning, but if you don't value yourself, you will never feel it. Remind yourself of your value and self-worth daily. I have my client keep all the letters, evaluations, and thank you cards from her students. When she is feeling unworthy, she goes through them and can see her value, and it reminds her of her worth.

Myths of Happiness

1. **Success comes before happiness**. Don't expect to be happier because you're successful at work, financially, etc. If we do this, we get caught in the cycle of "I will be happier when . . ." When I make more money, get a bigger house, get a promotion, finish graduate school, etc. We will always be on the search to get to a destination or reach a certain goal. Unfortunately, when we get there it's not usually what we expected or we have short-term happiness. We are happy first, then we feel successful.

2. **What's going on in your life is the cause of your happiness**. What's true is that how you *perceive* the events in your life is the cause of your happiness. Some of your circumstances might seem negative, but it's about how you view them. I had a client who got fired from her job. For most, that would be a negative situation, but my client saw it as an opportunity to start her own business.

3. **Happy people are always happy**. Happy people still have bad days and bad situations. We know life is a roller coaster ride and not a smooth ride. We expect the ups and downs of life. We don't expect a perfect life or strive to have one.

4. **Happiness doesn't affect your performance**. Actually, the happier you are, the better your brain works. A recent study at the University of Warwick found that happiness led to a 12% spike in productivity.

5. **Happy people are selfish**. People are afraid to work on their happiness because they think others will see them as selfish. The truth is the happier we are, the better we can take care of others and be there for our friends and family. We can't give to others

what we don't have. How can we be a positive parent if we aren't positive? How can we be that role model to our kids? How can we help others if we aren't emotionally and physically healthy? This is why making sure your basic needs are met is so important (Habit #1). The other part is that we are happy when we help others. When I'm in a bad mood, one of the easiest, quickest ways to get out if it is to help others. Kindness brings happiness.

6. **We don't like happy people**. I have heard that happy people are stupid or annoying. This is not true. Happy people are viewed as friendlier, warmer, less selfish, more confident, and even more physically attractive. Just another reason to go out there with a big smile!

7. **I don't deserve to be happy**. One of our biggest fears is that we're not worthy or not good enough. This is not true. We are all worthy of being loved and happy. We need to get back to a place of self-love. To practice loving yourself more, let go of what others think and be your authentic self. Stop comparing yourself to others, and let go of perfectionism and control issues; they both set you up for failure. Practice gratitude (Habit # 2).

Bonus Happiness Tips

1. **Socialization** is one of the main factors of happiness. Without socialization, we can feel lonely and isolated. Socialization consists of community, support system, and leisure. We need all three to be happy. We need people who we love and love us unconditionally; this is a basic emotional need. Family and friendships increase our overall happiness and meaning in life. Also remember, socialization can look differently for everyone. I have a client who is an introvert, so to her being social is spending time one-on-one in a quiet place. For an extrovert, it could be a concert or happy hour.

2. **Lifetime learners are happier**. If we continue to learn, both personally and professionally, we will continue to grow and develop. Otherwise, we can feel stuck. Every time you're feeling stuck or stagnate, try to learn something new. It can be done informally through a trip, tour, movie, book, discussion, etc., or formally through classroom training. It doesn't matter what or how you learn, just that you keep learning. A bonus of learning is meeting new people when we attend classes, events, etc. We can mix learning and socialization together and create more happiness in our lives.

3. **Have fun and be creative**. We need to play and enjoy ourselves. Make sure to add fun activities to your weekly schedule the same way you would schedule a play date for your kids or a doctor's appointment. It gives you something to look forward to.

4. **Live in the moment**. We are our happiest when we are in the moment. Savor the moment—relish in whatever you're doing. This could be taking a shower, eating a cookie, or having a cup of coffee. This means taking a few extra minutes to mindfully enjoy the moment and activity you're doing. Flow is another great way to be present. Flow is when you're so involved in an activity that you

lose track of time and everything around you. You're so focused on your activity that you don't pay attention to the distractions around you, like the phone ringing or the music blaring. I have had clients tell me that hours have passed while in flow and they didn't even realize it. Flow is an activity that challenges you but isn't too hard that it can't be done. It doesn't cause stress but instead causes you to grow.

5. **Learn from your past**. You don't need to forget it, but you don't want it to weigh you down. So, instead, use your past as a teachable/learnable moment and move forward.

6. **Plan for your future**. You can't control your future, but you can plan for specifics like retirement, college for your kids, and keeping healthy now so you're healthy later. Plan for what you can, then let go and enjoy what comes your way. Be open to the new possibilities and opportunities the future holds.

7. **Religion, spirituality, and happiness**—following a spiritual path or belonging to a religious organization brings social support, community, and friendship. Faith in a higher power (something bigger than ourselves); prayer and gratitude, which are meditative acts; and a commitment to community all lead to higher levels of happiness. One of the best ways to live a spiritual life is to be your authentic self. Be true to who you are and live your truth.

8. **Enjoy the journey to happiness**. Do some trial and error. A lot of my clients don't know what makes them happy; they know what makes everyone else happy, but not themselves. If you find yourself in this category, try new things and see if they bring happiness. If they bring you happiness, great. If not, move on to the next thing. Try to remember what brought you happiness before you got wrapped up in life. Some of those things could still bring you happiness, but you will never know unless you try. The journey of happiness doesn't mean every day will be filled with joy. We will still have bad days, but as an optimist, you will be

able to see the big picture and know that bad days don't last. Happiness is just around the corner.

9. **Don't judge yourself or others**. You can't be happy if you're in a state of judgment. Allow others the freedom to experience their own journeys, in their own way and in their own time frame.

10. **Take baby steps.** What are some little things you could do daily to make you happier? For me, its setting my morning intention of what kind of day I want, saying my morning thanks to others, and my gratitude checks. All of those actions take very little time and they are free, but those little steps make me feel happier because they are heading me in the right direction, to the person I want to be. What action steps can you take daily to be the best person you can be?

11. **Set realistic expectations**. Don't expect to always be happy. You will have bad days and times of stress. You will have days filled with "negative" emotions. This is all normal. Give up unrealistic expectations.

12. **We all have different happiness levels**. Some people are genetically more joyful than others, but remember we can always be happier than we are today. We also each have a different version of what makes us happy, different goals, and different ways to get there.

13. **We can control only ourselves and our reactions to others**. If we try to change others to help cultivate a happier life for ourselves or for the other person, we are setting ourselves up for failure. If you practice the habit of accepting and embracing change, this will release some of your stress and life will run more smoothly.

14. **Happiness is contagious** (and so is negativity). We can't change or fix others, but we can spread our happiness and positivity. We can influence other's happiness by our own mood. Just as someone's bad mood can rub off on you, so can a good mood. We can spread positivity. According to a study published in *Statistics in Medicine* conducted at Harvard University and University of

California, a friend who lives close to a happy person has a 25% higher likelihood of becoming happy, too. The spouse of the happy person has an 8% increased chance of happiness and the next-door neighbors have a 34% chance. When one person is happy, he or she spreads it to their friends and family, and it continues to spread to *their* friends and family. It's the ripple effect. Your moods do matter; your moods affect others.

15. **Never compare yourself to others**. It's a losing battle. When we compare ourselves to others, we cause feelings of envy, jealousy, low self-esteem, fear of missing out (fomo), and depression. We always assume the grass is greener on the other side, but the truth is we never know the true story of someone else's life. It might look great on the outside, but we don't know what goes on inside. When we power down from technology we help to remove unhealthy feelings of jealousy, envy, and comparing ourselves to others. We look at social media and think everyone's life looks better than ours and feel dissatisfied with our own lives. On social media, people tend to show the positives of their lives to others and keep the negatives to themselves. Instead, compare yourself to who you were. See how far you have come and what positive steps you have taken.

16. **Change is the one constant in the world.** We can't avoid change. The resistance to change just adds stress to our lives. The best way to reduce stress is to accept that change will happen.

17. **We can never be perfect**. Don't try; instead strive to be your best self. Trying to be perfect puts you on the road to a life of unhappiness. Perfectionism is a learned trait. The good news is it can be unlearned. There is a difference between high standards and perfectionism. Setting high standards for ourselves is good, but if we become obsessed over making mistakes, then we are striving for perfection. When we are so worried about our mistakes, we tend to feel that others will think badly of us. We are never completely happy with any of our tasks, and this can lead to

feelings of unworthiness or incompetence. Embrace your imperfections because they make you unique.

18. **Mindfulness cultivates happiness**. It makes us aware of the present moment. We are our happiest in the moment and fully enjoy what is going on at that moment. A friend of mine gave me a great example for this tip: "There were days when I'd go for a walk and have about a hundred things on my mind. Before I knew it, the walk was over and I wasn't able to enjoy it. The next time I took a mindful walk, I used my senses. I noticed the blue sky, the singing of the birds, the laughter of the kids at the park, and the smells of the barbecues, and the experience was much more relaxed and enjoyable."

19. **It takes two and a half to three months to create a new habit**. Have patience. If we give ourselves the time needed to form a new habit, that habit will become a lifestyle change.

20. **Money and happiness**—when we ask people what would make them happy, many mention money. The truth is more money doesn't bring us more happiness. As long as our basic needs are met, money doesn't make that much of a difference in our overall happiness. Money does affect our happiness if we use it to buy experiences and memories. For example, instead of spending money on a brand-new car, you could buy your family a trip to Italy for ten days, where you created memories and experiences that would last a lifetime. Another way to create happiness with money is to spend it on friends or family, or donate it to charitable causes.

21. **Aging and happiness**—this one surprises many. We think in the US that age is a negative, which makes us believe with age comes unhappiness, but it's not true. Great news for many (I'm in mid-life, so I understand how valuable this news is), we actually get happier with age. We have more positive emotions and fewer negative emotions, we care less what people think, and we are less sensitive to stress.

22. **Nature vs. nurture**—we have a mix of genetic and environmental factors in our happiness. Genetics is responsible for 50%, 10% is due to circumstances, and 40% (key number) is learned/environmental. This means 40% is in your control. It is determined by your actions and choices. That is huge. We are not victims of our DNA.

23. **Being happy with chronic illness depends on the ability to remain hopeful**. The chronically ill who are happy continue to set dreams and goals (even if they needed to be changed due to illness), realize nothing is perfect and are grateful for all the good in their life (gratitude), share their struggles, advocate for their illness, take their illness in their own hands, and have a good support system. They don't give up, and they are not victims. People who live with illness make this a conscious choice.

I hope these 23 tips help you to feel healthier and happier. They are all great ways to cultivate more happiness.

Happiness must be cultivated. It is like character. It is not a thing to be safely let alone for a moment, or it will run to weeds.

—Elizabeth Stuart Phelps

The Connection Between Mindfulness and Happiness

The three key components of self-compassion are self-kindness, a sense of common humanity and balanced, mindful awareness. Kindness opens our hearts to suffering, so we can give ourselves what we need. Common humanity opens us to others, so that we know we aren't alone. Mindfulness opens us to the present moment, so we can accept our experience with greater ease. Together they comprise a state of warm, connected, presence during difficult moments in our lives.

—USCD Center for Mindfulness

There are the basics of mindfulness that we all know. It reduces stress and increases well-being and happiness, reduces chronic pain, lowers blood pressure, boosts the immune system, helps us feel more rested, and helps us slow down and be in the present moment. That should be enough to want to meditate and live mindfully. Another reason is that anyone can do it, anywhere, at any time. It's free and has no side effects. One more reason is that happiness is an inside job; the best way to go inside and increase happiness is through mindfulness. Mindfulness trains the brain to be more positive and resilient.

People who are mindful are significantly happier because they stay in the moment. Most of us are on autopilot and don't pay attention to how much our mind wanders into negative noise. External gratification can bring some short-term happiness, but for long-term happiness we must go inside, and that's where mindfulness comes in. When we savor our positive experiences, we feel happier.

To be mindful means seeing the world with a fresh pair of eyes. We no longer see the world through judgment. We see the world through loving eyes. When we see the world through love, we are able to see all the beautiful things around us. We see all the things we tend to ignore and not appreciate, and we spend time in the present moment without past baggage weighing us down or feeling anxious about what could lie ahead. This definition can help us to see how mindfulness helps us to cultivate a happier lifestyle.

When we see the world through love, we reduce our decisions based on fear. We make better choices, choices that are healthy and true to ourselves.

We tend to see beauty when we are mindful. We can see beauty in nature just by talking a walk or spending time at a park. During this time, we are in awe and wonderment of the beauty that surrounds us. We feel a sense of gratitude for all of nature and what it brings to us. These positive emotions help us live longer and be happier and healthier.

Mindfulness slows us down to enjoy our lives, to be in the present moment, to be focused on the activity or the person in front of us. We feel the hot water on our back from the shower without rushing or worrying. When we are mindful, we actively listen and have better conversations. We are not thinking of our past and the regrets. We are not worrying about the future and causing anxiety by what-ifs. Instead, when we are mindful, we choose to be in the moment. We are our happiest in the now. When we are in the now, everything is fine. It's when we focus on the past or future that we start feeling anxious or depressed.

Mindfulness makes us more self-compassionate, kind, and accepting. When we don't accept ourselves, we are being judgmental and harsh, making ourselves feel worse. We beat ourselves up instead of being kind and compassionate, but mindfulness stops the negativity by stopping the judgment and comparison of others. We remove the unrealistic expectations of ourselves and accept who we are. As more mindful, compassionate people, we realize our happiness is related to the happiness of others. We feel a connection to all other humans and animals. When we help others, we find true happiness. Positive psychology states that one way to be happier is to perform random acts of kindness. This would become part of our daily life if we lived more mindfully, and we would be in a state of kindness and compassion. Mindfulness creates a more empathetic brain. It makes us understand others' pain and suffering. What I have seen is that when people become more mindful, they are able to relate to others' emotions. Even if I haven't been through what someone has been through, I can still understand their pain and suffering because we all have struggles and negative experiences that have caused us to feel pain and suffering. When we are empathetic, we can relate to the emotions and understand how those emotions can affect someone's life. This empathy makes us want to help.

Another connection is flow. Flow is a positive psychology word coined by Dr. Mihaly Chentmihalyi. Flow cultivates mindfulness. When we are in a state of flow, we are fully in the present moment and meaningfully connected to the activity. It's when you give your full attention and concentration to an activity that you do for intrinsic reasons (for your own sake). You are totally absorbed in the activity, and everything is working well. You're not thinking about it; it just flows. You're not judging every move you make or even planning; you're just going with the flow. In flow, your ego takes the back seat and everything just flows. You forget about time, hunger, any plans you had, any pain you're feeling, or any outside activities or worries you have. You have no sense of time. It just flies by. When in flow, our brain waves operate similarly to when we meditate. Flow creates happiness but is also a state of mindfulness. People say they are in flow during sports and physical activities, while they perform artistic and creative activities, and when they listen to music, have a meaningful conversation with a friend, garden, etc.

Cultivating a Mindful Lifestyle

When I first learned about mindfulness, I thought it was meditation. That is just a small part of what living a mindful life is about. Mindfulness is a way of life: a realistic, peaceful way of life. It's something I have striven for, but couldn't quite obtain, especially being a "type A" personality living in the suburbs of NYC. I thought, "How could I ever live a mindful life?" It seemed so impossible to be a mom, a wife, *and* a part-time college professor while running my own business full time. I kept asking myself the question over and over again: "Is it possible to live a mindful lifestyle?" And even though I wasn't sure at the time, I somehow knew it was a possibility. So, I went on the journey of finding different ways to add mindfulness into my life and create the life I always wanted, full of peace and happiness.

What Is Mindfulness?

Mindfulness is being in the present moment, observing your thoughts and feelings without judgment. It's being awake and aware of new possibilities, clues, or signs of which direction to follow. Mindfulness is being in the moment to clearly see those signs and clues, and to hear your intuition.

It's awareness of the present moment and how you are feeling, without judgment. When you're in a state of awareness, you have the ability to respond with clarity. You can notice if the decisions and choices you are making are coming from a place of love or fear.

Mindfulness means looking at situations with kindness and compassion, including your own situations. This seems to be the hardest challenge for most.

The Difference Between Mindfulness and Meditation

Meditation and mindfulness are always discussed together, and they should be; mindfulness and meditation complement each other. But they are different.

Meditation is a practice, something we set time aside to do frequently. It's a practice or technique that focuses on the development of concentration, clarity, and a state of calm and peace. There are many different types of meditation. Mediation is time that you set aside to practice. It can't be done all day, every day because we need to live, work, play, etc.

Mindfulness is a general awareness of everything around you. It's slowing down and being in the moment. It's a way of life because we can be mindful in any daily activity. We become aware of each moment by intentionally paying attention without judgment. The other day, I was doing laundry and decided to do it mindfully. With each piece of clothing I picked up, I took a few seconds to hold on to it and feel the warmth. It was such a great experience on that cold, winter day. Just feeling the warmth, smelling the freshness, and feeling the texture of the soft, cozy blanket made doing laundry a little easier and more enjoyable. It turned a mindless activity into a mindful one.

Benefits of Mindfulness

1. The more mindful we are, the more we live in the present moment. We are our happiest when we are in the moment. We worry less about the future, which eases stress.

2. We become aware of our mind-body connection, which allows us to feel where we hold negative emotions in our body. This allows us to use the connection as a warning sign/red flag that something is wrong, which allows us to make changes.

3. We slow down and enjoy life. We start to enjoy the simple things such as a conversation, nature, our friendships, the sunset, etc.

4. We become aware of the beauty that surrounds us and we connect to nature.

5. We become aware that everything is love. We need to give love and receive love in order to be happy.

6. We increase our self-awareness, which can help us become aware of our limiting beliefs and change our negative thinking and behaviors.

7. When we live a mindful life, we realize everything is temporary. So, even when times are tough, we know they shall pass. Mindfulness allows us to see the big picture in life and not get stuck on the small things. We all could use that reminder now and then.

8. We become more focused and engaged in activities.

9. Both our mental and physical health improve. Mindfulness lowers blood pressure, reduces stress, and eases chronic pain.

10. Our sleep improves.

11. We gain acceptance of our situations. Mindfulness allows us to stop resisting and let go of fighting the things we can't change, which reduces stress. When we are mindful, we feel the resistance and can work on where the resistance is coming from and why it's there. Resistance can show you the fear and doubt you have been holding onto. Resistance is a sign of staying in your comfort zone, which can lead to feeling stuck and stagnate. When we are mindful, we are feeling. The feeling might be discomfort—which is a sign of resistance, but it is also a sign to dive deep into that feeling and stop it from taking over.

My Wake-up Call

I was having a typical Sunday, with nothing special going on. I was watching Super Soul Sunday (on the OWN Network) and a segment appeared about a man, his dog, and saying good-bye. Usually, I shut these types of segments off because they bring too much sadness and loneliness from another chapter of my life that I lived through many years ago but still have an emotional connection to. This time was different. I reminded myself to be mindful and stay in the moment, to be awake and aware of what I was truly feeling. So, this time, I left the segment on and cried hard for about twenty minutes straight. For me, this was huge. If you knew me, you would know I rarely cry. I sometimes feel that crying means I'm weak. (I know logically that this isn't true, but learned habits can be hard to break.) For me, crying was a release I never allowed myself. This time I did. I didn't even know how much I needed this release until it was over.

Mindfulness taught me that we need to feel more, even if those feelings are sadness, hurt, pain, grief, anger, or loneliness. Most of the time, when these emotions come up, we try to avoid them by occupying ourselves. We run away from the feelings. This stops us from truly feeling the emotions and finding a sense of relief and peace. By staying mindful, we can feel these emotions and even stay in the feeling for a little bit until we slowly feel better. When being mindful, we don't push to feel better or say, "Time is up, time to move on." We don't set any expectations or time restrictions. We just go with the feeling; when we feel it, we can heal it. I want to say that again because it's such a powerful statement. "When we feel, we can heal." When we hide from our emotions, we never get the chance to be in the feeling and heal. These emotions will keep rearing their ugly heads until we acknowledge them and pay attention.

Mindfulness will not let you ignore what you need. Mindfulness is a reminder to pay attention to what you're feeling. Mindfulness teaches you to ask questions such as:

What emotion am I feeling?

What are these feelings trying to tell me?

What do I need?

There is a reason for your feelings: baggage that comes up with these feelings, a story we need to listen to, and a part of our soul we need to heal.

After the mindful moment passes, you will feel either more relaxed or more drained. Pay attention to what your body needs after this emotional moment. This is called the mind-body connection. Our bodies tell us what we need, whether it's more sleep, relaxation, food, water, etc. Most of the time, we don't pay attention to this connection. We say we don't have enough time, or it will pass. The truth is, these physical signs are red flags telling us to take action and make changes. After a mindful moment, we have more clarity and less judgment toward ourselves and others. Take advantage of this time to sit for a few minutes alone and write down your thoughts and needs. Then follow your own advice. When you listen to your body, you can be in better health, both physically and emotionally.

Once a week, stop for a few minutes and check in with yourself. I have my clients spend a few minutes alone to check in with themselves. Most of us know where we hold stress in our bodies, but when you check in, ask yourself where you're holding stress. Sometimes it spreads. Our typical areas where we hold stress are:

- Stomach—a client of mine expressed it best. She said it feels like someone is inside your stomach wringing a wash cloth.
- Headaches/migraines.
- Jaw pain from grinding or clenching our teeth, which can also cause ear pain, tooth pain, and/or headaches.
- Neck and shoulder pain from tensing up.
- Low immune system—you catch every cold, flu, or virus that you encounter.

- Joint pain throughout the body.
- Change in your sleep and eating habits.

When you are aware of the areas where you hold stress, it can be a little easier to check in. I also have my clients ask them themselves some simple questions:

How am I feeling?

Where have I been holding stress? Is this my typical area, or is it spreading?

What am I stressed about? What changes can I make to release some of the stress, both physically and emotionally?

What is one thing I can do today to relieve some of the stress? This can be as simple as taking a walk, talking to a friend, taking a bath, deep breathing, yoga, massage, etc.

Mindlessness

One way to become more mindful is to notice when we are mindless. Another way to think of mindlessness is when we are on autopilot, when we are zoned out. When we are mindful, we are zoned in. When we are on autopilot or zoned out, we are not in the present moment. We are our happiest and most mindful when we are in the present moment. Start noticing when you are mindless. When you become aware of your mindless activities, you can change and be more aware and present.

Some examples of mindlessness:

- In the middle of a conversation, we zone out. Sometimes we assume we know what the other person will say or we don't like what we are hearing, so we zone out and don't even hear what he or she is saying.
- When we multitask and try listening to someone, we usually don't remember the conversation. One time, when I was driving home from work and talking on the phone, I was focused on driving and the traffic, what I would make for dinner, and what happened during my day. When I arrived home and ended the conversation, I realized I had no idea what we just talked about.
- When we drive to a place frequently, we end up zoned out while driving. How many times have you made it home and not remembered stopping at the stop sign or passing the local store at the corner of your block?
- We walk into a room and don't remember what we were coming in for (I do that often).
- We forget where we put things. I still remember a client coming in for a session very upset, looking for her sunglasses. She couldn't find them. They were on the top of her head.

Mindfulness Techniques

If you want to conquer the anxiety of life, live in the moment, live in the breath.

—Amit Ray

Active and Empathetic Listening

Active Listening

When people first hear this, they don't get how this is a mindfulness technique, but it's a good one. When we are an active listener, we are fully involved in the conversation. We are in the moment and being fully present for the other people involved.

Most of us only listen halfway. This can cause a lot of problems. When we listen to others, we are thinking about how to answer, we interrupt to answer, or we are thinking about something else. When we listen only halfway, we make assumptions about what someone is saying or assume we have heard it before and answer inappropriately, which can cause a disagreement or hurt someone's feelings. When we are not an active listener, we don't pay attention to our own non-verbals (body language and facial expressions), and we don't pay attention to others'. Non-verbals can add a lot of information to a conversation. If we are not being an active listener, we tend to not see these actions. It detracts from our understanding. When we aren't actively listening, others can see it on our faces. We might look away, roll our eyes, or have that distant look when we have left a conversation mentally. Active listening shows the other people involved that you are truly listening and that you care. This can change the dynamic of a conversation for the positive and cause less disagreements.

Here are a few easy ways to be an active listener:

1. Make eye contact.

2. Don't interrupt. Allow the person to finish before answering.

3. Take some time to pause before answering in order to think about your answer.

4. Watch your non-verbals and tone of voice.

5. Pay attention to others' non-verbals.

6. Ask questions if needed.

7. Express your interest with facial gestures.

8. Consider your technology. If you are constantly paying attention to your technology, you are not actively listening, and it shows. You might simply turn it off.

These few, easy listening tools can become habits in a few months and change the way you have conversations.

Empathetic Listening

Empathy is a learned trait. If you're not an empathetic person by nature, there is no need to worry. You can form this great habit. A lot of us become empathetic because of situations and tragedies we have been through. There is nothing like hitting rock bottom to develop empathy.

Empathy is putting yourself in someone else's shoes. It doesn't mean you have necessarily been through the same thing or can even understand it. You can imagine and, to a point, understand what that situation has caused, such as pain, suffering, loss, anger, etc. We all know what it feels like to have those types of emotions, even if it's for a different reason. This is what connects us and makes us all human.

When we pay attention and listen to someone with an empathetic ear, we hear differently. We hear the emotions and how much they are affecting that person. It makes us want to reach out and be there for the other person, to give them love, kindness, and caring. Empathy brings us back to times when we have felt lost, empty, and alone.

When we listen with an empathetic ear and an open heart, we can help someone feel valued and heard. Empathy allows the person to know they are loved and cared for. This allows the person to be vulnerable and begin to heal.

Here are a few ways to be an empathetic listener:

1. Imagine how the other person is feeling. Try to put yourself in their shoes and imagine the emotions they must be feeling, even if it's a situation you have never been through.

2. Tell someone you can only imagine how they are feeling. The truth is, we never know exactly how someone is feeling. Even if we have been through the same tragedy, we all react differently.

3. Show you care with empathetic non-verbals, such as a tender touch, a hug, eye contact, and nodding to show you're listening.

Change the Words, Change the Conversation

We must be mindful of how we speak, what words we use. For example, what if we decided to change our wording when it comes to being angry? We use the word "mad" to describe how we are feeling when we are angry, hurt, or in an argument. What if we switched our word from "mad" to "sad"; would that change the dynamic of the conversation? When you define the word "mad," what comes up for you? When I hear that word, I immediately become defensive. I get into argument mode, where I become aggressive, feeling like I'm at war or in battle. When I think of the word "sad," I get a totally different feeling. Sad makes me feel that someone is in pain, hurting, or suffering. I think they need help and warmth. That is a completely different feeling than "mad" brings. Both still bring up emotions, but with "mad," I think war and battle; with "sad," I feel the person still cares and is just struggling. Feeling that someone is sad or mad sets a clear tone for the type of conversation we will be having. I think "sad" is a better choice; it still gets the point across that someone is hurt and unhappy.

Just being mindful of the type of words we use can bring a totally different outcome in a conversation or send us in a different direction. This is the case with so many words. If we watch the wording and the tone of how we say things, we can prevent a lot of arguments.

It's also how we speak to ourselves. Are you using words like "should," "could," "would," "can't," or "maybe"? When I use phrases like "I can't" or "I should," it's stating that I won't with an excuse. Similarly, when someone uses the word "maybe," including myself, I know it means "no." Watch what you say and how you say it. Choose wisely.

One Thing at a Time—Life Is Not a Race

In today's rush, we all think too much, seek too much, want too much and forget about the joy of just Being.

—Eckhart Tolle

We are a society taught to multitask. If we are not doing more than one thing at a time, we are failing. We need to be constantly on the move and getting things done. We are taught that if we take too many breaks, relax, and stop for a while, we are lazy and unproductive. Well, that is just not true. If anything, it's harmful to our health. Many of us have become type A personalities. Living in New York for most of my life, and then its neighboring state New Jersey, I have grown up with the traits of a type A personality. These traits include being competitive, impatient, fast paced, and controlling as well as having a short fuse, easily snapping at others, always feeling a sense of urgency and becoming irritated, expecting and trying to achieve perfectionism, and being a workaholic. I felt guilty if I wasn't working or being productive. I felt like I always needed to be "on." This is an unhealthy way to live. It causes us to be stressed out, showing signs of stress by grinding or clenching our teeth, not getting enough sleep, high blood pressure, heart disease, and even social isolation. We need to stop this behavior and slow down.

A great way to do this is to stop multitasking (at least most of the time) and become mindful of where you put your attention and focus. I know sometimes it's impossible, but if we think about it, we can slow down and not multitask at least half the time. This would, at the very least, give us a break. When we do one thing at a time, we can give it 100% of our attention. It gets the time, attention, and focus it needs. The outcomes are better. We are more productive and creative for each thing we do. It takes away the added pressure and stress from ourselves and our bodies.

I have my clients write out what needs to be done each day, and its priority. The priorities need to be done that day and the rest can be moved to the following day if necessary. Each item on the list needs to be done without anything else going on. Sometimes you need to take a few minutes to look at the list to realize you're setting yourself up for failure. We create these unrealistic lists that don't involve eating or sleeping. This will make us sick in the long run. If the list is unrealistic, then it's time to look at the big picture and start removing or reducing some responsibilities. We need to learn to delegate and say, "No." These are tools to release our control. We mark off each time something gets done and take a few minutes in between each activity to notice how well we did it and how we are feeling without multitasking. Every time we feel the good mood and see the productivity, it motivates us to continue living this type of lifestyle. Make the mindful choice of where you want to put your attention and focus. If one had three things to do, a mindful person would pick one and put the attention on that task and when done go to the next task. Mindfulness is a lifestyle choice.

The Negatives of Multitasking

1. We work fast and miss important information. We increase the rate of error in our tasks.
2. We lose productivity and become stressed.
3. We forget things.
4. We are not giving each task 100%, we are not fully committed to any of the tasks, and it shows in the end result. Then we feel guilty that we didn't do a good job from the beginning.
5. We get easily distracted with everything else around us. It takes us time to get back to the task, which means we wasted time.
6. We are not in the present moment when multitasking, which makes it much harder to problem-solve and be creative.

Choose Love

Hatred never ceases by hatred; it only ceases by love. This is a timeless truth.

—Joseph Goldstein

Ask yourself: "Am I making each decision or choice from a place of love, or fear?" When you have conversations that are getting heated, or you are already in the middle of the debate or voicing your opinions with attitude, ask yourself, "Am I showing love or fear? Am I coming from a place of love or fear?" If we are being judgmental, we are coming from a place of fear. "Am I looking to prove myself? Do I need to be right?" That's more fear. I have made a mindfulness choice for myself. I always want to come from a place of love.

Take some time when making all choices and decisions to really think about the question. If we make choices and decisions based on love, we can eliminate guilt and shame. Our decisions and choices will steer us in the right direction. We are a society based on fear, so naturally we see and feel fear around us. The media makes our fear even stronger. We see fear all throughout media and society. Fear leads us into wrong choices that are based on looking for acceptance and approval from outside of ourselves (which is setting ourselves up for failure). Many are choices that hurt ourselves or others and can bring us, and others, pain and suffering. Love would do the complete opposite. Paying attention to the question ("Did I make this decision based on love or fear?") before we jump at a decision will cause a huge shift in our life. Just that one simple question can change the direction of your life.

If you realize you're making decisions based on fear, ask yourself: "How could I make a more loving decision? How can I add more love and compassion to my life?"

We have the power to follow the path of love. Life is based on the sum of our choices. Choose love!

God-incident

I must give my friend Diana the credit for this section. She introduced me to the god-incident. There is no such thing as a coincidence. It's all a path/plan laid out by your higher power. When we are mindful, we will look at every incident and see what is truly going on. When we realize this, we can start asking ourselves the question "What is the reason for this situation?" Sometimes the question can take months or even years to answer, but there is always a reason and lesson to be learned. Sometimes the lesson is patience. Patience in the situation, patience for learning the lesson and making the changes. Patience can be tough, but with patience comes growth. Sometimes the lesson isn't for you; you're just the helper and the lesson is for the other person. Sometimes our biggest failures, mistakes, and/or challenges lead us to the right path, and without that God-incident, we would remain stuck in the wrong direction and not growing. Our biggest challenges can be blessings in disguise. If we can remember that everything happens for a reason, we can start looking for the lesson.

The biggest lesson I've learned is that everything has a purpose and we can be divinely guided in the right direction. All of this made me realize that no matter what situation I was involved in, no matter how painful it was, I was never alone. I always had a higher power guiding and watching over me. This was a comforting lesson to learn. I would never have learned this without slowing down and being more mindful. We need to be open and looking for signs. When we do have the God-incident or sign, we follow it. Sometimes the sign will cause a life-changing event; sometimes it's a sign you're in the right direction or the wrong direction, or it's an encouraging message. We need to be mindful to see the signs and to remain open. Mindfulness will help you to remain open, to see yourself with love and compassion.

We must realize faith is a partnership between us and the source (higher power). It's saying, "I will do the work down here on earth, if you can cleanse my soul to have more room for healing, forgiving, and being a better, kinder, more patient person."

Simplify Your Life. Isn't It Time to Decrease Emotional Clutter?

Emotional detox is cleansing the toxic people and situations from your life. Moods and emotions are contagious, so if we surround ourselves with toxic people, we can become drained, exhausted and negative.

What Is a Toxic Person?

There is a difference between a negative and a toxic person. It's important to know the difference. Everyone will have bad days and go through tough times. When someone is in the midst of a challenging time, they might be negative. This person will be negative but not take it out on you or make you feel worse about yourself. You will know that this person is loving and kind, and just going through a tough time. There are also people who are just generally negative; they see the world through the glass half empty belief system. These people can be pessimists or some will call themselves realists. These negative people can still be good friends, show they care and be there for you in times of need.

Then there is the toxic person. Toxic people are destructive and exhausting. Toxic people create a lot of drama in their lives or surround themselves with drama, or both. They can be manipulative and controlling, self-centered, and narcissistic. They can be overly critical of themselves and others, and are typically very jealous. They don't like when others do well and can't be happy for others. They detest genuine happiness. Toxic people don't take responsibility for their lives; they are perpetual victims. When you spend time with a toxic person, you feel worse than when you arrived. When we spend time with toxic, unhealthy people, we feel drained, exhausted, and unhappy.

What is toxic for me might not be toxic for someone else. Everyone has different patience levels and a different past. Our past can affect our relationships of today. For example, if my mom was a very selfish person and it caused problems for me as a child, I might be set off by people who are selfish. For someone else, selfish might be annoying but not that big of a deal. We have to listen to ourselves and our bodies. We can feel when someone is toxic to us because we feel the physical effects. I know if I'm around someone who is toxic for me because I feel like my stomach is tied in knots. If I get a phone call or text from a toxic person, I can feel it in my stomach. Use your physical signs as a red flag to help you determine who is toxic for you. I have a client who expressed the need to take a nap after spending time with a toxic family member. I had another client tell me she would leave with a pounding headache after spending time with a toxic friend. These are definite signs that the relationship is toxic and a sign that you need to break off the relationship or create as much distance as possible.

8 Signs of a Toxic Person

1. Lying—a lot of toxic people are frequent liars. A healthy friend is someone you can trust and be your authentic self around. If you notice frequent lies toward you or others, it's a sign.
2. Jealousy—do you find this person to be unhappy for you and any of your accomplishments? This is a sign. A person who truly loves you wants to see you happy and wants you to succeed.
3. Victimhood—if someone is always the victim, they are not taking responsibility for their actions. A victim will take much more then they will give. Walk away.
4. Gossiping—frequent gossip is a sign. If someone is always gossiping about others, they are probably gossiping about you. Don't you want people in your life who show respect for others?
5. Number one—a toxic person put themselves first every time. They are taking much more than they are giving. This is the person who

usually doesn't even ask how you are doing or show concern for your well-being. They talk much more than ask questions. They lack empathy and compassion toward others.

6. Complaining—we are not talking about the person who is going through a tough time, we are talking about the constant complainer. They might even blame you for not helping them enough. Nothing you do will be good enough. They hate everything and find the negative in every situation. If someone's negativity is getting in the way of your happiness, it's time to move on.

7. Arrogance—do they think they are the best in every situation? The smartest? That they are always right? Do they constantly put others down? Never consider anyone's point of view but their own? Do they have to win in every disagreement?

8. Hurtful—they will say things to hurt you or disregard your feelings. If you find yourself being hurt frequently or your feelings often being pushed to the side, it's time to see the signs—it's toxic!

Do an emotional detox and remove toxic people and situations from your life. If you can't remove them totally, then make sure to set up boundaries and limitations that are healthy for you.

First, we need to know what the limits are. Know what you can tolerate and accept. Also, know when you have had enough. What does that feel like for you? I had a client describe how when things were becoming overwhelming and stressful, her shoulders and neck would tense and the beginnings of a headache started. That was her sign that her limits had been met and it was time for her to set up a boundary or leave the situation totally. If we don't set up limits and boundaries, we start feeling resentful.

Once we know our limits, then we should create the boundaries. Setting a boundary could be saying, "No," which can be tough for many. Remember that saying no and setting the boundary is really just a sign of self-respect and self-care. For some, setting boundaries can involve the length of time we spend with a person. Others are able to communicate the boundaries. You create the boundaries that work best for you. I had a client who set very clear boundaries with a friend. She would only see this person once a season for dinner. She knew that was all she could handle. I had another client who had a family member who was toxic, and she would only see this person in groups—not one on one.

You also have the option of removing toxic people from your life. Yes, you can break up with friends, co-workers, neighbors, even family, but it's a choice. If you have people who are toxic and who you haven't broken up with, you need to ask yourself, "What need of mine is being met?" We sometimes keep toxic people in our lives because it meets our own needs. I used to keep toxic people in my life because these people were so unhappy and made their unhappiness so clear, I took it upon myself to help them. The problem was, these people never asked for help and didn't want help or to change. It was my need. I wanted to help them. The key factor here was that it was my need, not theirs. I needed to learn that not everyone wants change or help. Making that assumption was only hurting me. When I came to this realization, I was able to walk away from the toxic relationships. I was becoming their personal therapist. It was becoming *way* too draining for me. This can lead to one-sided relationships. When we are in a one-sided relationship, we can feel trapped in the relationship, feel drained and exhausted after spending time with that person, and find ourselves constantly making sacrifices. We can put ourselves in the position to be the caretaker or the giver. We set little or no boundaries, are people-pleasing, have a lack of communication of how we are feeling, and become dependent on the relationship due to a fear of being rejected or feeling lonely or abandoned.

It's up to you what boundaries or limitations you set up or if it's better to end the relationship. When we remove the toxic, we remove the drama and the negativity. That is a huge weight lifted off our lives. Be mindful of the people you choose to be part of your life. As I said before, moods and emotions are contagious. It's hard to be at peace when you're surrounded by negativity.

If choosing to remain in a toxic relationship or feel you have no other choice than there a few things you need to do to remain healthy.

1. Don't expect change or try to change them. Truly accept the person for who they are.
2. Set distance. Don't get too involved with the person's problems. You can listen, but remember toxic people don't want solutions, they just want to complain. After listening to someone complain for a few weeks, it becomes more stressful to you, the listener.
3. Surround yourself with positive people to balance out the negativity.
4. Don't get wrapped up in their negativity. Remember to remain focused on compassion, empathy, respect, and love.
5. Don't take it personally. Their negativity is a reflection of them, not you. They act this way to everyone. Don't react to their negativity and rudeness.
6. Focus on you and your growth. Remain focused on what makes you happy and your value system. Stay true to that.

Fillers

Don't fill your day just to be occupied. This is just being busy for the sake of being busy. Instead, spend as much of your time as possible doing things that you love and enjoy, or that give you a sense of purpose. Make a list of five to ten things you love to do, and incorporate them into your weekly schedule. Don't waste time and energy on activities that are just fillers. When we do that, we feel empty.

Busyness can be used as a defense mechanism. It helps us avoid our own thoughts, feelings, and fears. When we finally take time to do nothing, we can confront our fears, feel our emotions, and work through them to get to a healthy place. I have a client who fills her days with shopping and lunch dates with people she doesn't enjoy, but she is so fearful of spending time alone that she just fills her time. The problem with this is that she still feels lonely and empty at the end of the day. Instead, spend some time alone to find out who you are and what you love to do. Spending time alone doesn't mean busying yourself with technology. It means finding solitude. Instead of having filler time, make a date with yourself to do things you love.

*Remember, solitude is different than loneliness. Loneliness is an unpleasant feeling. When we are lonely, we can feel sad, isolated, depressed, and/or abandoned. With solitude, we're alone but it's a positive time where we can reflect, recharge, and heal/grow.

Doing Nothing

This might sound crazy, but yes, I want you to spend some time each day just doing nothing. For most of us, that will feel very awkward and wrong. It can be downright uncomfortable. Again, if we are type A personalities, this will go against everything we have been taught to do. No matter how it makes you feel, I want you to do it anyway. Step outside your comfort zone and spend some time doing nothing—and this means nothing. It doesn't mean taking a nap or a walk. It means just sitting and observing. A lot of my clients will say sitting in nature is the best way to do nothing. Concentrate on your breath or a noise around you to stop the constant chatter in your mind if possible. If not, just let the thoughts flow, observing them. Don't judge or answer them. You don't want a full conversation going on inside your head. If you do that, you won't get the sense of peace and stillness. You will only get more noise.

I have my clients do a simple technique to clear their mind and give themselves a little break from work. Sit down in your chair, hands on your lap, close your eyes, and take a few deep breaths to relax. Then count slowly in your head up to thirty or forty. When we count, we don't pay attention to the other thoughts going on. After you count to thirty or forty (if you even get that far), you start to drift and end up in a state of stillness that can last for a few minutes. Enjoy it. Do it a few times a day if you need. Every time we take a break from the norm, we get a chance to be in the moment and relax, which clears our minds and allows us to refresh and refuel. When we come from these breaks, we are more productive and creative. So, taking a two- to three-minute breather can actually help with your job or schoolwork.

Trying to do nothing is tough at first. We will crave busyness. We have so much going on in our lives between, work, family, school, etc. Then add technology into the mix, and we never have to be alone or do nothing. Doing nothing will feel uncomfortable for most. Schedule some down time where you have nothing to do.

Stillness

One of our basic needs is stillness. We can get stillness in various ways, such as nature, meditation, and prayer. It doesn't matter how you find stillness; it's just important you have stillness in your life. Without stillness, we feel spiritually starved. We can't sift through the noise in our heads to hear our inner voice. We can't find a place of peace and calm.

I often get asked how I find stillness. It's different for everyone. I feel solitude and peace when I'm walking in nature, but what works for me might not work for you. Try walking, sitting in nature, meditating, or prayer. They are all good options, but I find one of the best helps is asking your higher power for help. Ask for the patience to be still. Don't go overboard with your expectations. If you can have stillness for two to three minutes a day to start, that's great. Make a commitment to yourself to be still for a few minutes each day. I spend my first few minutes asking for guidance and then just sitting in silence in nature. I have clients who will create stillness in their car when driving by shutting off the radio and cell phones. It doesn't matter how you do it or when; just make it part of your daily routine.

Just Breathe

Each day, take a few minutes to just breathe. When we do this, we slow down and clear our minds from the chatter.

Practice breathing in through your nose, holding your breath for a few seconds, then exhaling through your mouth. Repeat this a few times. You will feel a sense of peace and calmness, and it reduces any physical stress symptoms. I do this exercise every time I get in my car at the end of the workday. It de-stresses me as I start my commute home to enter the next phase of my day, family time. You can also do the 1-2-3 technique. To start, inhale for a count of three, then hold for a count of three, then exhale for a count of three then repeat. I repeat the 1-2-3 technique a few times until I feel more relaxed. This can be done anywhere at any time. It's simple and helps to relax, especially if we are nervous.

Unplug

Technology has both positives and negatives, but too much technology can cause us to feel disconnected from life and stressed out. We need to have times in our day where we are tech free to disconnect from all the clutter in our lives. Everyone has their own times, but for most it's nighttime. If we can shut our phones and computers down a few hours before bed, we will sleep better. Another important tech-free time is during dinner. We should not have our phones or TV on while we are eating. This time is quality time for families and is meant for conversation, not staring into technology. For me, time adds pressure, so I made Sundays my tech-free day. I don't even wear a watch most Sundays (unless I have a special event). Time can add pressure and a sense of urgency that causes stress. To be more mindful, we can't multitask. Unfortunately, most of us try to live our lives working, studying, socializing, doing housework, etc., while paying attention to our technology. It overstimulates us and takes away from the activity at hand. The other day, I was on social media while I was supposed to be working. I thought it was for 30 minutes or so, but when I finished, I realized I had spent over an hour on social media. I felt unproductive and guilty for wasting so much time on the Internet when I had so much else to do. Due to the long break on social media, I had a hard time getting re-focused on work and my assignments took me an extra two hours.

Benefits of Tech-Free Time

- This gives us time to disconnect, relax, and refresh. We need to set boundaries with work and have time that we are not available for work. In the end, we will be fresh and recharged for the next work day. It benefits both the employee and employer.
- We can become addicted to the Internet. When we spend too much time on social media, we can become obsessed and end up

scrolling mindlessly for hours. This takes away from our productivity. I have had clients who feel guilt for spending so much time on the Internet and others who start comparing themselves to others on social media. It makes us feel connected, but we are not having face-to-face interaction. This can cause jealousy, envy, and loneliness.

- *To realize how addicted you are to your technology, leave your smartphone home for the day or a few days. Turn off your tablets and computers and see how you feel. I have had many clients who can't function without the smartphone and feel anxious all day. Sounds a little like addiction.
- When we shut off technology, we can enjoy the present moment. Let's face it, whether we have smartphones, tablets, or other devices, life is still happening around us. The more time we spend plugged in, the more we miss out on life. We have new experiences every minute of the day, and we could be missing so many of them due to being plugged in. I see so many people at concerts, dinners, etc., and instead of enjoying the moment, they are busy on technology. They miss out on all of these wonderful experiences that you can't get back.
- A bonus from unplugging could be saving some money at the end of the month. It was not the reason my clients unplugged, but it was a bonus.
- Physical benefits—better sleep, less neck pain, less eye strain, fewer headaches, improved memory, and a lift in spirits. The less time we spend plugged in, the more time we have to relax, focus on enjoyable activities, spend time socializing, and have new experiences. More bonuses to unplug.

Be Aware of the Task

When we slow down during each task and stay in the moment, we can appreciate and find enjoyment in the little things. Mindfulness means being fully aware of every moment, even the simple things we do daily. It means being aware through all your senses.

Here are some great examples:

- While taking a shower, just be still under the hot water and feel the water touching your skin and the sensations it causes. Hear the water fall like rain drops. Enjoy the steam. How does it make you feel?
- Walk everywhere slower. When I leave any store, I walk slow to my car. I walk slow into my work. How do you feel when you slow down? What do you notice around you? The slower I walk, the more I notice nature and the sights and smells around me.
- When eating, slow down and chew your food numerous times. Feel the texture. Notice the colors on your plate, the aroma coming from your meal. Enjoy the taste. While eating with others, don't eat and talk at the same time. Put your fork down while talking.
- One of my clients swears that slowing down has changed how she does the dishes. She no longer uses the dishwasher. She loves to feel the warm water and suds on her hands for a few minutes before she even touches the dishes. I haven't reached this bliss yet, but you get the point. J

Nature

When we feel connected to nature, we tend to feel more inspiration, awe, wonderment, and peace. These positive emotions cultivate happiness. Surround yourself with nature as much as possible. This can be hard if you live in cold areas during the winter, but try as much as you can to bring nature to you. This might mean having indoor plants, bright open windows with plenty of sunlight coming through, looking through the window to admire the snow falling, or having a pet. These can bring a sense of nature to us all day.

- What do you see when you open your windows? Being surrounded by nature is a great way to get a boost. In the winter, I can look outside and see the trees, grass (or snow), and bushes.
- We can decorate our houses with bowls filled with rocks, pebbles, stones, or a tabletop water fountain. The gentle sound is very soothing. Stop and get flowers on your way home to liven up the house during the winter months.
- Having a bowl on the kitchen and dining room tables filled with colorful fruit or fall veggies, such as pumpkins and squash, will give us a feeling of the nature of autumn.
- Place a bird feeder outside your window so that you see and hear the birds when you wake up.
- Nature-themed artwork can bring in the nature feeling.
- Taking a walk in nature will help you to be in the present moment and enjoy your experience. Using your senses, what do you see? Hear? Smell?

These are just a few ideas. Get creative, use your imagination, and have fun! Of course, any time you can spend time outdoors with the fresh air and vitamin D, do it!

Don't Overthink

Overthinking is a natural part of life and affects all of us at different times in our lives. Overthinkers are more prone to sadness, impaired problem solving, negative thinking, and low motivation. We naturally judge and label. You want to stop this habit. So, instead of judgment and labels, be more kind and compassionate. This includes to yourself.

Ways to Stop Overthinking

1. Don't strive for perfection—we tend to constantly think about a situation if it's not perfect, but all that is doing is setting yourself up for failure. Perfection is impossible, so let it go. It will just stress us out to try and reach something that we can never reach.
2. Time limits—I allow myself to overthink or even sulk for a little bit, but I always have a time frame. I might allow a pity party for the day, but the next morning is a new start and the pity party must end.
3. Talk to yourself—every time I have a negative thought, I say the word "no" or "stop" to myself. It's a sign to stop the negative self-talk. I then ask myself why the thought isn't true or realistic. I replace the negative thought with a positive one. After all the self-talk, take some action.
   Examples: If I find myself having negative self-talk about being loved, I will take action by calling or spending time with people who make me feel loved and cared for. If I find myself saying that I'm a failure or nothing good happens for me, I will write a list of all my accomplishments to see how far I have come.
4. Stay away from triggers—what situations and people make you overthink? If we know our triggers, we can prepare and plan for them or avoid them completely. Instead, try to surround yourself

with people who make you feel good. Read and watch things that make you feel good and produce positive thoughts.

5. Be more mindful. There is no right or wrong way to be mindful or to meditate. When we think there is, we detract from the experience. Don't look at mindfulness as a chore. It's a state of being. It's enjoying and feeling alive in every moment. It's being fully engaged in every activity and conversation. When we are in the moment, we are not worried about the past or the future.

Remember, every moment of your life is important, no matter how big or small.

Live Intentionally

Living intentionally means taking some time to reflect on your values, opinions, and priorities. It allows you to figure out who you are, the "why" behind what you do, and who you want to become. It means living with clear intentions and purpose.

Let's start by asking yourself:

1. *What's my life vision?* To live intentionally, you have to know what type of life you want. You create the life you want. You can't create something if you don't know what that is. Create your vision first. What does your life look like? What does it feel like?

2. *What is my purpose or main goal in life?* When we know why we do things, we become more motivated to do them, or to be a certain way.

3. *What type of person do I want to be? What type of personality traits do I want to have?* Think in terms of being a role model to your kids (real or imagined). What traits do I want them to have? For them to have those traits, they must learn them through observation and role modeling. Good news, you're the role model.

4. *You are responsible for your life and your life only.* Don't try to create anyone else's happiness but your own. The good news is your happiness and mindfulness will help and impact others as a natural side effect of your own work.

5. *The choice to live intentionally means being your true self.* It means being open and brave. Your intentions might be different than the intentions others have for you. That's OK. Continue on *your* path. It is your life, and you have to live with the choices you make.

6. *What is my value system?* Does the life I live represent my values? Am I setting goals that are in alignment with my value system and my authentic self? If not, what changes can I make starting today?

7. *What are my core beliefs?* Do these beliefs hold me back? Are they limiting my life? If they are, it's time to create new beliefs. Your core beliefs are repetitive thoughts and assumptions you think about yourself, others, and the world around you. These beliefs can be based on your upbringing and not even be your own beliefs. They are learned. These beliefs don't have to be true. Remember, any thought we constantly repeat to ourselves, or hear from others, becomes a belief, but that doesn't make it factual. For example, "I'm ugly," "I'm fat," "I'm stupid," etc. Our core beliefs become who we are and dictate how we live our life.

Some questions to ask yourself to find out your core beliefs:

Do I think I am confident?

How do I look? Do I think I look pretty, ugly, fat, thin, and/or mediocre?

Do I judge myself constantly? How?

Do I feel worthy of love? Happiness? Success?

Do I feel I am inferior or superior to others?

Do I think everyone around me is luckier, or has a better life?

Do I feel smart or stupid?

Do I see life as good or bad? How do I view the world?

Can I see both the good and the bad in the world? In people? Situations?

These questions will help you become aware of your inner beliefs and help you recognize them. Start paying attention to your self-talk. When a situation arises that causes you to feel sad, upset, angry, disappointed, etc., what are the first feelings or thoughts that pop up? Those are your inner beliefs. When you can't fall asleep at night, or wake up in the middle of the night with all the self-talk playing in your head, those are your inner beliefs. How do you handle mistakes or failures?

Write down these core beliefs and evaluate them. Are these beliefs holding you back? Are they true? Consider where they come from. A lot of our beliefs are not our own. Are they even coming from a reliable source? Your beliefs can be the voice of your parents, ex-spouse, old boss, etc. When you can see where they came from, decide if they are limiting or not. This can help you make changes and remove those beliefs and form new ones. Challenge the old limiting beliefs and create new, more positive, beliefs. Your core beliefs form the foundation of your life, how you live life, and your overall happiness.

What Do You Value?

What do you value? It's important to live our truth, which means being true to our value system. I realized one of my values was to not hurt others intentionally. If I was aware of a situation that caused pain to others, then I needed to stop and make a change. I realized that I wasn't always living up to this value. My behaviors weren't always matching up to my value system. It was causing my soul to drag. The only way to find true joy was to make the changes necessary to live my truth.

Make a list of your values. What do you value/what's important to you? Are you living in accordance to your value system? If not, what changes can you make? For me, every time I'm in a situation or faced with a choice/decision, I always ask myself, "Does this choice or decision allow me to be the best person I can be? Is my behavior/action matching my value system? Am I living my truth?" If the answer is no, I will spend some time figuring out why I made those choices or behaved those ways. What was I truly afraid of? By doing this, we are becoming aware of our fear and can make better choices. Awareness is key to living more mindfully.

A lot of my clients have a tough time thinking of what they value. Here is a list of values, but there are so many more. Take some time to think about your value system.

Values

Knowledge, education, Lifelong learning

Strength, physical challenges

Fun, amusement

Altruism

Assertiveness

Beauty

Bravery, courage, daring

Community, friendships, relationships

Personal growth

Environment, nature, animals

Money, wealth

Advancement and promotion, status, fame

Religion, spirituality

Peace, calm, serenity

Security, stability

Family

Happiness, joy

Time, freedom

Showing Compassion

We use the word "sorry" to express our condolences for a loss, but the most powerful act of compassion and empathy is touch. Being mindful can help us realize and be aware that words are not always enough. Physical affection allows someone to feel loved and comforted without judgment. It takes away the worry of having the perfect words. There is power in touch. When we don't know what to say, we can express our love, sadness, empathy, and compassion through our tears, a soft touch, a hug, or a kiss. Others can feel the compassion and love through touch. When we use touch, we give the gift of ourselves, the gift of our heart and love. Always extend a helping hand, smile to all, give your time and friendship to people who are feeling alone, show expression of love and concern to people who are in a state of worry and fear, and share hope and inspiration to all who feel hopeless and helpless.

We can show compassion through touch but also through empathy, listening, kindness, and unconditional love. It's making the choice to see the good in others, in the world.

Gratitude and Random Acts of Kindness

Be kind whenever possible. It is always possible.

—Dalai Lama

Gratitude is one of the best tools we have access to on a daily basis. It's free, simple, and not very time consuming, yet the benefits are huge. It puts us in a state of mindfulness, which boosts our emotional wellness.

Gratitude can be used as a form of meditation. You can repeat "thank you" as the mantra in your meditation.

You can make a conscious choice to be more mindful of all the good in your life, to be mindful when someone is kind to you or goes out of their way to show love. We can get so caught up in life that we fail to see all the kindness.

We went over gratitude in one of the beginning chapters of the book, but just a quick review. Make gratitude checks a habit. Take a few minutes each day to ask yourself, "What am I grateful for?" You can write down, say out loud, or think to yourself two or three things you are grateful for. I want you to be very mindful when thinking of what you're grateful for. These don't have to be big things. The small things are just as, and sometimes more, important.

I do my gratitude check every morning in the shower. I start my day with gratitude so it will put me in a good state of mind. It puts me in a mind of appreciation and thanks for all I have. While in the shower, I say to myself, "What are two or three things I am grateful for?" I visualize all the negativity going down the drain. You can add any visualization to your gratitude check to enhance it. I do it in the shower because the shower is a relaxing time. The heat and steam relaxes me. It's private and it doesn't interfere with my schedule. I would shower every morning regardless of my gratitude checks, but these checks have become a daily habit.

- Be careful of the gratitude trap—if you notice you're saying the same things every day and it becomes autopilot, you won't get the same results. This is a sign of being mindless. If you find yourself in that cycle, pick one thing each day you're grateful for and then ask why. The why asks you to dig deeper.

Give gratitude to others, which is also a random act of kindness. Once a week, I try to say a thank-you to someone in my life by sending a text, email, or calling and just saying, "Thank you for being a good friend" or "Thank you for being in my life." It's something small but meaningful. Again, this won't change your schedule or take up too much time, but it can make a difference in your life and the life of someone you know.

Every time we perform a random act of kindness, it's a win-win situation. The person doing the act of kindness gets a boost of happiness. The person you do the act for receives a boost of happiness. Everyone is a winner. The other great side effect of acts of kindness is the boost of self-esteem for both participants. The only thing to be careful of is your ego. A random act of kindness is done because you want to do it from your heart, not for a response or a thank-you. If done for the wrong reasons, you can end up feeling worse. Do a random act of kindness with no expectation. Do as many as you can, as often as you can.

I always imagine a world where each person does one random act of kindness per day and how it changes the world drastically. Think about it and start today.

Miracles

A miracle is defined in the dictionary as "a surprising event that is not explicable by natural or scientific laws and is therefore considered to be the work of a divine agency." It really is a change in perspective, a shift that causes an "aha" moment.

Pray, meditate, and ask for a miracle, but be aware that the miracle might not be what you wanted or expected. Be mindful of what you're asking for, but then let go of any expectations. We need to look past our own wishes and desires to see what a true miracle is. What we think might be the best isn't always. We need to leave the decision-making of a miracle to a higher power. Mindfulness teaches us to not hold onto things and to not be attached to any expectation.

We can spend months and months praying and meditating for a loved one to be at peace and free of pain. In our minds, that might mean the miracle is a new cure or treatment, but instead the person passes on. We get angry and blame the higher power, but didn't a true miracle just happen? The person is no longer in pain or suffering. They are now in a place of love and peace. Isn't that what we asked for?

We must put our own desires aside to see what's truly best for the other person or for ourselves. If we are praying and meditating for a miracle and guidance, then we must trust that our higher power knows better than we do. We must remember what we desire might not be the miracle the other person or we needed. The higher power can see the big picture, which sometimes we are too blind to see.

Miracle exercise: At the end of each day, write or say two or three miracles that happened today. A miracle could be anything. We see miracles every day; it's just taking the time to notice them, to be more mindful of everyday miracles. A daily miracle could be birth, healing of an illness, a rainbow, the unconditional love of an animal, a flower blossoming, seeing a car accident where no one gets hurt, seeing a butterfly in the middle of a cold, snowy winter, etc.

Are You Truly Living?

To truly live, I mean really live, we must be in forward motion. It means growth. This means being of service each and every day through your purpose and passion. Let's be mindful of life and living authentically.

Start with the question "What is the legacy you want to leave?" That legacy should be what you're working on daily. A legacy is not just what you want to leave when you die, it's how you want to live each and every day. It's how you want to affect people today. You want to cause positive change not just when you're gone but while you're alive. It's living in alignment with your values. The foundation of your legacy is built while you are living.

You want to ask yourself:

> *What will I leave with others today and when I'm gone?*
>
> *How will I touch and inspire others?*
>
> *Am I passing along my true values and beliefs?*

You want to be conscious to how life unfolds. The questions below will help you be more aware and live authentically.

> *What if you looked at every situation or issue as a way to let you know it's time to make a change?*
>
> *What if you looked at problems and difficulties as opportunities for spiritual growth?*
>
> *What if the people who push your buttons were sent to you to give you a lesson?*
>
> *Are you settling for a life that was chosen for you by your parents or society? But you crave more?*

Do you see your mistakes and failures as teachable, learnable moments?

To create the living legacy, start by asking yourself:

What would I like to change or improve in this world? Whether on a big scale or within my own circle, or both?

What do I want to be remembered for? What message(s) will I leave?

What actions do I need to take?

If I were born again, would the life I just lived be an inspiration? Would I be a good role model for my new life?

Live in the Moment

The way to live in the present moment is to remember that this too shall pass. When you experience joy, remembering that this too shall pass helps you savor the here and now. When you experience pain and sorrow, remembering that this too shall pass, reminds you that grief, like joy, is only temporary.

—Joey Green

We are our happiest when we are in the now, but our mind wanders to our past and anticipates our future. Both types of wandering can add to our stress. When we get stuck in the past, we can feel a loss of identity, a loss of time, regret, anger, etc. When we anticipate the future, we create worry. We can't control our future. Trying to just sets us up for failure. Living in either the past or the future can cause us to feel "stuck." We can't move forward living in the past or the future. We need to be in the present. The present is where we feel our best.

I want you to use your past as teachable and learnable moments. Don't forget your past or you will continue to repeat over and over again the behaviors that caused you pain and stress. Instead, look at every past failure and mistake as a teachable moment. We can notice when our past haunts us by how much we repeat the same words, habits, or patterns. When I start to feel stuck and I pay attention to what my inner dialogue is, I notice it's a lot of noise. A lot of my past comes up, which leads me to worry about my future. When I pay attention to this noise and allow it to take over, it causes a lot of stress and fear. We have a choice to shut off the noise and come back to the present.

A great mindfulness technique I use when I have too much noise is to quiet myself and take a few deep meditative breaths while sitting outside in nature, or if the weather doesn't allow it, I sit at a comfortable spot where I can view nature from inside. I focus on something out in nature such as the birds singing, hearing the wind breeze through the trees, or watching the clouds move and the shapes the clouds form. I notice the different colors of the flowers blooming during springtime or the different colors of leaves falling in autumn. Each time can be different. Focusing on something in nature helps you to connect with yourself and quiet your mind.

Once you quiet the noise and gain a sense of stillness and peace, you want to ask yourself the following questions to help you learn from your past:

> *What can I learn from my past mistakes/failures? What are the lessons?*
>
> *How will I grow from these lessons?*
>
> *What changes can I make?*

You can't predict your future or control what will happen, but you can prepare. For example, we set up a 401K for our kids' college education, we set up an IRA for our retirement, we start to exercise, take vitamins for our health in the future, etc. There are certain things you can do to prepare for your future, but that's about it. Prepare and then release the rest and come back to the present.

We can do grounding exercises to remind us to stay in the moment. Below are a few. Try and see which ones work best for you. They are all simple and can be done in times of stress or nervousness, or when you need a reminder to be in the moment.

1. If you are feeling stuck, change your position. Wiggle your fingers and toes, shake your hands, or stamp or tap your feet. Pay attention to the movement. This wakes you up to being in the here and now. I have clients who will pinch themselves or wear a rubber band and snap it to remind themselves to get back in the present.

2. Pick up and hold an object that comforts you, such as a stuffed animal, smooth stone, or a piece of jewelry. Some of my clients

play with their necklace or bracelet, or a stress ball. Use anything that works for you.

3. Use your voice. Say, "I am here in this moment." "I'm aware of everything around me." "I'm awake and in the present."

4. Write out what's going on at the moment. Keep writing without judgment or any type of spelling or grammar check. Use this as a release. Keep writing until you feel a sense of release, relief, or both.

Get off of Autopilot

After my vacation, which happened to be over the New Year's holiday, I made a mental list of the small changes I wanted to make in the New Year and started these changes while I was away. They included less technology and eating healthier.

I figured I had a good start, but when I walked in the door of my home after vacation was over, my old habits came right back. Within a few hours of being home, I noticed myself sitting in my bed on social media while snacking on chips. What I realized is that as soon as I got home, I went right back to autopilot. I was just doing without awareness. I did my old habits without thinking. It was right then that I realized the real small change (not that small, but doable) I needed to make was to become more mindful—to pay attention to what I was doing. Instead of living on autopilot, I need to live in the present moment and be conscious of what I'm doing and why. Once I'm aware of what and why, then I can make the changes I needed.

So instead of spending time on social media, I took out a book that I have been wanting to read and took a nice hot bath. As for the snack, I realized I wasn't hungry and didn't need to eat at 8:00 p.m. If I had been in the present moment, I would have said no to the chips.

Instead of being on autopilot, be aware, awake, and mindful by paying attention to your daily routine and asking yourself, "Is that what I really want to be doing?"

Momentary Moments

Momentary moments bring us boosts of happiness. They are taking some time to enjoy the simple things in life. It's like the cliché, "Stop and smell the flowers."

Example: It could be something as simple as enjoying your cup of coffee in the morning. I used to drink my coffee every morning while getting ready for work and getting my daughter ready for school. I drank the coffee, but it was an afterthought. I never fully enjoyed it or even remembered the taste or smell of it. Now, I do my mornings differently, even if it means waking up ten to fifteen minutes earlier. I make my coffee while sitting in the kitchen, just enjoying the aroma. I don't do anything else. I just relax and enjoy the aroma of the coffee. I take my cup of coffee and either sit outside on my deck (weather permitting) or I sit in my family room on the couch gazing outside the window, watching nature and enjoying my cup of coffee. This gives me a few minutes to enjoy my cup of coffee, relax, and enjoy time with myself. I can get lost in my thoughts or just have a clear mind and allow whatever thoughts or observations come my way. When I'm outdoors, I enjoy nature, the sun rising, the dew on the grass, the smell of the flowers, and the birds singing. All of it is quite peaceful.

What are some simple things you love to do but don't fully do? For example, taking a walk, sitting in a bath, reading a good book, etc.

A momentary moment means to savor the moment. Be in the present and enjoy it. When we have momentary moments, we cultivate a feeling of happiness.

Get off the Hedonistic Treadmill

We get so wrapped up in material stuff, we don't spend enough time truly focusing on the important things, such as friendships, experiences, activities that cause flow, friendship, nature, and animals.

We need to stop focusing on the material. It's OK to have material items, but when we stay focused on them and expect the material items to bring happiness, then it becomes too much. When we buy something material, such as a piece of jewelry, a new car, new coat, etc., we get a high that feels good, but it's short term. It could last for a few weeks to a few months, but it's only temporary. If we look for our happiness to be found this way, we are setting ourselves up for failure and will be stuck on the hedonistic treadmill. This means we will continue to have to buy things to support our happiness. Once the happiness of the bracelet you bought fades, it becomes, "What's next?" We start needing the next best thing. We get stuck in the "I will be happy when . . ." syndrome. I will be happy with the new bracelet, but then I need the matching earrings and then the ring and so on.

It also creates a feeling of keeping up with the Joneses, of needing to compete and constantly compare myself with others. If my neighbor has the new sports car, then I need one, too. If my neighbor's kids have the best new sneakers, then I need to get them for my kids. This has put America in huge debt. That causes us Americans to live in constant stress and worry. The only person you should do better than is yourself.

Ask yourself:

> *How can I do better today?*

> *How can I be a better person then I was yesterday?*

Never look for acceptance and approval from others or compare yourself to others. It's setting yourself up for failure.

Just Feel

Feel your emotions. We need to feel to heal. If we push problems aside, or occupy ourselves instead of feeling, those problems come back and rear their ugly heads at a different time. If we stay in avoidance and resistance, we don't feel the emotions that allow us to heal and move forward. If we don't feel the emotions, we can't take action. If we don't feel the emotions, we won't understand where all the pain and fear is coming from. We won't express or work through it. It's hard to make good decisions if we don't understand what we're feeling and why. We must not judge our emotions, which we tend to do.

I hear women say, "I can't show anger. It's not attractive for women." I had a woman client tell me that her husband says how ugly she looks when she is mad. Men feel they can't cry to release their emotions. It will take away from their masculinity or they will appear weak. The truth is, there is nothing weak about feeling and expressing emotions for both men or women. Anger is a natural emotion for both genders, and to push it aside because you're a female will just cause more pain in the end. The best way to deal with this is to just feel your emotions, releasing them the best way possible for you, and to not judge. If you feel your emotions and start understanding them, you will see why you feel a certain way and what you require to meet your needs. You can start understanding that underneath some emotions, like anger, is fear. You can start processing the fear, but you can't do any of this unless you feel.

I'm not saying to feel and then react. Our feelings can cause us to make decisions based on fear: to overreact, to jump at situations, or to act irrationally. What I mean is feel it, observe it, and express it so you can make a rational decision based on clarity. If your feelings become overwhelming, then it might be wise to feel with some guidance from a professional. If not, then you can express it through various ways such as:

- Journal writing—writing your feelings out.

103

- Talking it out with others.
- Meditating/praying on it—bringing a higher power into the process.
- Crying, screaming, hitting a pillow, etc.
- Releasing your emotions physically through exercise.

Be mindful. Pay attention to your feelings and how you are feeling physically. Observe these feelings. Feel them, but don't judge. Just feel. Learn a lesson from the experience. Make sure to take deep breaths through this process. Some of my clients like to make the commitment to release the feelings. They will say it out loud or write it down. "I'm letting go of_____." I had a client who was holding onto anger for being cheated on. When she was done feeling, she made the conscious choice of releasing the anger so it would no longer be in power. She expressed this choice by saying it out loud to herself, and to me, as a symbol of moving forward and releasing the past. You can find your own releasing ritual.

It's important to feel safe with feeling and expressing. If you are going to open up to someone and be vulnerable, make sure it's someone you trust and feel safe with. Sometimes we don't need a solution. Sometimes we just need to feel and then heal. Healing takes time. Be patient and kind to yourself through the process. Be mindful of how you treat yourself (especially the inner dialogue). This is a time for self-care. A true good friend or family member will let you know you're heard and loved. Sometimes, that's all we need.

If you don't have a trusting, safe place to open up, a professional or spiritual counselor can be an option. Other options are shown above. If you write it out, you can still release your feelings. If you're afraid someone will read it, you can rip it up or delete it. It doesn't need to be saved for it to be effective.

Remember, it's important to feel the feelings, not just talk or write it out. Feel it with whatever process you choose.

Another option is to look at the consequences of not feeling. When you repress your emotions, you end up feeling or experiencing:

1. Mental and physical fatigue.

2. Depression.

3. Troubled relationships.

4. A lack of motivation or caring.

5. Irritability.

6. Feeling tension and anxiety throughout your body.

7. Decreased immune system.

8. A wide variety of health problems.

9. Using substances (drugs and/or alcohol) to numb the pain.

Each morning we are born again. What we do today is what matters most.

—Buddha

Mindfulness Exercises

I give a few different mindfulness exercises below that either my clients or I use. There are a few mindfulness exercises in the readings, also. This gives you many choices. Pick and choose the ones that work for you. I find all of the exercises to be an easy way to get back into the moment even when I'm busy with life. The great news is any activity can become a mindfulness exercise. You can practice mindfulness throughout your whole day.

1. Every few hours, take a few minutes to breathe and check in with yourself. How is your body feeling? Are you feeling stressed? Worried? Just being aware helps. If you notice tension, then you can take the next step to release it through stretching, walking, yoga, sitting in nature, etc.
2. Quick count—I have my clients at work or school sit down with eyes closed and take a few deep breaths. Remain seated with eyes closed, start counting to yourself very slowly from one to fifty. Most clients tell me they zone out around the thirty mark. When you zone out, stay for a few minutes relaxed.
Option 2—breathe in through your nose for a count of three, hold for a count of three, and release your breath through your mouth for a count of three. Do a few of these breaths to slow down and relax physical anxiety symptoms such as your heart racing or chest pounding.
3. See both sides of the coin—think about some situations in your life that you're not very happy and satisfied with. Take a few minutes to notice why you're not happy. This will be the easy part. Now take a few minutes to notice all the good about the situation, the "silver lining." When I was first diagnosed with my serious, chronic medical condition, I was very focused on the negative.

Then I took a few minutes to find the silver lining and it amazed me to see all the good. The illness forced me to change my diet and I lost some weight, had more energy, and now have a healthier lifestyle. The illness educated me on invisible illness, and I was able to cultivate more empathy. I was able to understand and work with people who had chronic illness. It opened up a whole new world for me. Don't get me wrong, I wouldn't wish my incurable illness on anyone, but I can definitely see how much I have grown and learned from the experience.

4. Mindfulness exercise with animals—as long as you have a safe furry friend, this exercise is great and your pet will love you for it. It's my favorite and my dog's, too!

   Start by stroking your pet with your eyes open for a few minutes. Than close your eyes and continue to stroke your pet. Feel the fur, the soft texture, how it feels on your fingers. Stay there for a few minutes and you will notice yourself being in the moment. Make sure that during this exercise you're giving 100% full attention to your pet and the experience.

   *Remember animals can teach you a lot about mindfulness—they live in the here and now.

5. Mindfulness break—take a few minutes to just gaze out into nature even if it's from your window. Pick something to look at, such as the leaves blowing, a squirrel running up the tree, the birds flying overhead, or the shapes of the clouds. Notice the colors, patterns, textures, etc. Be observant, but don't label or judge. This gives you mind a break from the daily grind.

6. When you find yourself in a stressful situation, such as waiting in line, sitting in traffic, etc., smile. Just smiling makes us happier and it brings us back to the moment.

7. Mindful eating exercise—mindfulness can go hand-in-hand with eating, too. It is very common for people to eat mindlessly, out of habit, boredom, avoiding feelings, stress, or any other reason that isn't actual physiological hunger.

   The next time you find yourself snacking mindlessly on chips as you watch TV or read, stop and ask yourself, "Why am I eating these chips? Am I really hungry?" If you are just snacking out of habit, or any other reason but hunger, stop. If you are truly hungry, and truly want to eat chips, put a small portion of chips in a small bowl instead of eating it out of a bag mindlessly. Mindless eating also leads people to not stop eating until the bag is empty. I've often had clients tell me that they don't even realize they are eating as many chips as they are, and are often surprised when the bag is finished. This is where mindfulness while eating can be helpful. Mindful eating involves using all of your senses while eating. It helps you to stop and pay attention in the moment. Since we're already talking about chips, I'll use chips in this exercise, but it can be done with any food. Here's what you do: take one chip out of the bag. Look at it. What do you notice? Do you notice its shape, color, crevices, etc.? Perhaps you see how thin or thick the chip is, or the little speckles of salt. Next, smell the chip—can you smell the oil, potato scent, or any spices? What does the chip feel like? Is it rough or smooth? Take a bite of the chip. Move it around in your mouth and notice how that feels. When you start to chew it, what does that sound like? What does it taste like? Swallow the chip. Do you notice you feel more satisfied eating it mindfully instead of mindlessly?

I don't expect you to eat your food with this much intention, and this slowly, each and every time. But the point of this mindfully eating exercise is to see how slowing down and paying attention, using all of your senses, will help you savor your food, and pay attention to how hungry or full you feel. Food is meant to be enjoyed, and practicing eating mindfully can add joy to your life. Further back in the book, we mentioned how doing one thing at a time helps with being mindfully happy. The same can apply to eating. The next time you are eating dinner at home in front of the TV or on social media, try to just eat and do nothing else. See how satisfying mindful eating can be.

Thank you to Dina Kimmel for her input on the mindfully eating exercise.

Dina Kimmel, RD, is a registered dietitian in New Jersey. She can be reached at dinakrd@outlook.com.

Notes

Mindfully Happy Habit # 1 – Are your basic needs met? Page 6

1. Leann Garms (Feb 9, 2012) Is stress making you sick? https://www.hoag.org/news/is-stress-making-you-sick-/

2. Kavitha Kolappa, David C Henderson and Sandeep P Kishore. No physical health without mental health: Lessons unlearned? https://www.who.int/bulletin/volumes/91/1/12-115063/en/

3. Andrew Soergel (Jan 12, 2015) Study suggests correlation between heart health and optimism, smile it'll make your heart happy. https://www.usanews.com/news/newsgram/articles/2015/01/12/study-suggests-correlation-between-heart-health-and-optimism

Myths of Happiness – Page 34

1. Jonha Revesencio (July 22, 2015) Why happy employees are 12% more productive. https://www.fastcompany.com/3048751/happy-employees-are-12-more-productive-at-work

Bonus Happiness tips – Page 36

1. Michelle Schoffro Cook (Oct 31, 2013) Study: happiness sis contagious. Https://www.care2.com/greenliving/study-happiness-is-contagious.html

About Diane Lang—Therapist, Author, Educator, and Life Coach

Diane has dedicated her career to helping people turn their lives around, and she is now on a mission to help them develop a sustainable, positive attitude that can actually turn them into optimists.

Through her two books, *Creating Balance and Finding Happiness* and *Baby Steps: The Path from Motherhood to Career*, Diane has been speaking to and empowering people nationwide. Diane is also an adjunct professor in Psychology at Montclair State University, where her college work includes mentoring students for personal issues and career advisement.

As an expert in her fields of therapy, Lang has been featured in the *Daily Record, Family Circle Magazine, Working Mother Magazine, Seen* on NJ 12 TV, *Good Day CT, Style CT*, The Viera Network, CBS TV News, and *Fox and Friends*. In addition, Lang writes a blog for pazoo.com.

For more information, please visit her website at www.dlcounseling.com or email Diane at DLcounseling2014@gmail.com.